HGTV
HOME & GARDEN TELEVISION

Sensible CHIC

SMART STYLE ON ANY **BUDGET**

MEREDITH® BOOKS   DES MOINES, IOWA

HGTV SENSIBLE CHIC

EDITOR Amy Tincher-Durik
SENIOR ASSOCIATE ART DIRECTOR Doug Samuelson
CONTRIBUTING WRITERS Judy Friedman, Susan Kleinman, John Loecke
CONTRIBUTING ART DIRECTORS Chris Conyers, Chad Johnston, Beth Runcie, Joe Wysong, Conyers Design, Inc.
CONTRIBUTING STYLIST Cathy Kramer, Cathy Kramer Design
CONTRIBUTING PROJECT DESIGNERS Sonja Carmon, Patty Mohr Kramer, Gayle Schadendorf, Jilann Severson
CONTRIBUTING PHOTOGRAPHERS Ken Gutmaker, Jay Wilde
ILLUSTRATIONS Rita Lascaro
COPY CHIEF Terri Fredrickson
BOOK PRODUCTION MANAGERS Pam Kvitne, Marjorie J. Schenkelberg, Rick von Holdt, Mark Weaver
EDIT AND DESIGN PRODUCTION COORDINATOR Mary Lee Gavin
PUBLISHING OPERATIONS MANAGER Karen Schirm
CONTRIBUTING COPY EDITOR Elizabeth Havey
CONTRIBUTING PROOFREADERS Carol Boker, Julie Cahalan, Beth Lastine
INDEXER Kathleen Poole
EDITORIAL ASSISTANT Kaye Chabot
COVER PHOTOGRAPH Ken Gutmaker

MEREDITH® BOOKS

EDITOR IN CHIEF Linda Raglan Cunningham
DESIGN DIRECTOR Matt Strelecki
MANAGING EDITOR Gregory H. Kayko
EXECUTIVE EDITOR, Denise L. Caringer

PUBLISHER James D. Blume
EXECUTIVE DIRECTOR, MARKETING Jeffrey Myers
EXECUTIVE DIRECTOR, NEW BUSINESS DEVELOPMENT Todd M. Davis
EXECUTIVE DIRECTOR, SALES Ken Zagor
DIRECTOR, OPERATIONS George A. Susral
DIRECTOR, PRODUCTION Douglas M. Johnston
BUSINESS DIRECTOR Jim Leonard

VICE PRESIDENT AND GENERAL MANAGER Douglas J. Guendel

MEREDITH PUBLISHING GROUP

PRESIDENT, PUBLISHING GROUP Stephen M. Lacy
VICE PRESIDENT-PUBLISHING DIRECTOR Bob Mate

MEREDITH CORPORATION

CHAIRMAN AND CHIEF EXECUTIVE OFFICER William T. Kerr

IN MEMORIAM E. T. Meredith III (1933-2003)

All of us at Meredith® Books are dedicated to providing you with information and ideas to enhance your home. We welcome your comments and suggestions. Write to us at: Meredith Books, Home Decorating and Design Editorial Department, 1716 Locust St., Des Moines, IA 50309-3023.

If you would like to purchase any of our home decorating and design, cooking, crafts, gardening, or home improvement books, check wherever quality books are sold. Or visit us at: meredithbooks.com

For more information on the topics included in this book and the show *Sensible Chic*, visit HGTV.com/sensiblechic

CONTENTS

Welcome to the World of Sensible Chic

Since its debut on HGTV, *Sensible Chic* has been a source of inspiration, giving viewers a glimpse into homes meticulously decorated by professional interior designers who use opulent antiques, one-of-a-kind artifacts, custom-designed furnishings, and luxurious fabrics. By examining the decorating and design principles employed to create these stunning interiors—with seemingly unlimited budgets—guest designers teach viewers how to get a high-end look for much less. Whether you are a fan of the program *Sensible Chic* or you are just looking for great decorating ideas that suit your lifestyle—and your pocketbook—this book will arm you with the knowledge to take what you see on TV and transform your own home into a Sensibly Chic masterpiece. Turn the page to enter the budget-savvy world of smart, sensible design.

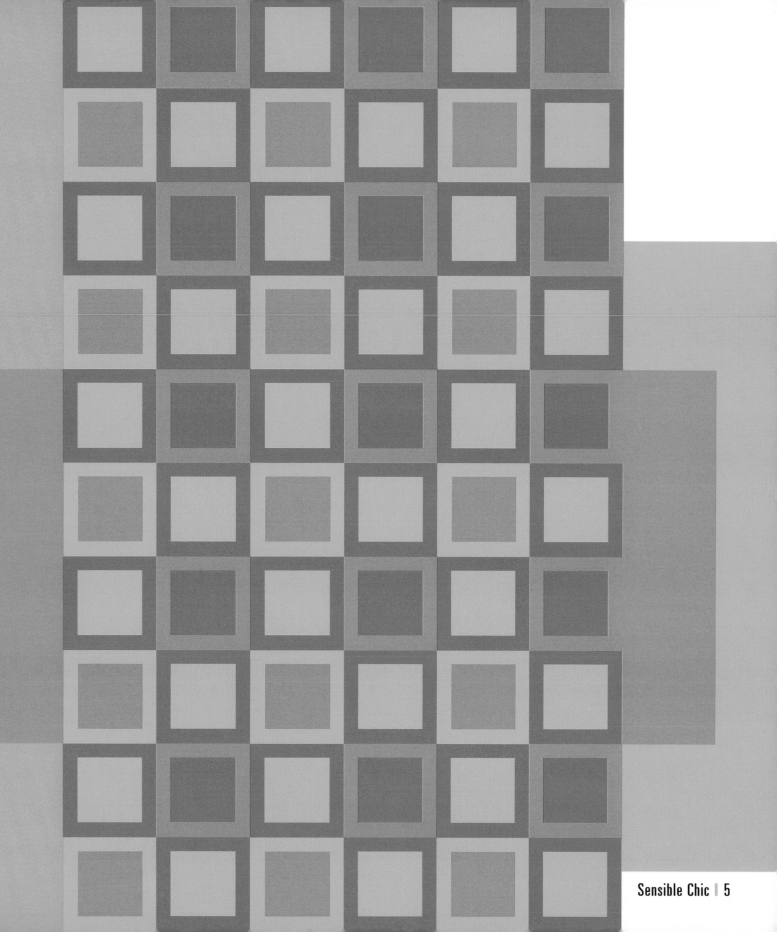

INTRODUCTION

If you don't have tens of thousands of dollars to redecorate any given room of your home, don't worry. The *Sensible Chic* experts are here to show you successful strategies for re-creating your space. From planning and shopping to fabricating custom projects, their methods are high on style and easy on your wallet. So check out this introductory section: It gives you a glimpse at the techniques they use to turn high-cost decorating dreams into a budget-friendly reality you'll enjoy for years to come.

Getting a fashionably chic look in a master bedroom can be achieved on a budget with off-the-rack window treatments and bedding and by sprucing up an old dresser with paint—or you can spend significantly more for custom-designed curtains, bedding in luxurious fabrics, and one-of-a-kind antique furnishings. The inspiration room right was created for $36,500, while the Sensible Makeover above came in at just $1,490.

SECTION 1:
Sensible Solutions for Decorating Dilemmas

Decorating a room isn't as straightforward as just bringing in some furniture, hanging a few prints on a wall, and maybe adding a lamp and calling it quits. To compose a room that's truly functional, looks great, and is a pleasure to be in, it takes time, planning, and an understanding of design and decorating principles professional designers use. While designers often work with clients who have large budgets for their room makeovers—as is evidenced by the inspiration rooms featured on *Sensible Chic*—it doesn't take big bucks to make an impact on a space if you utilize the right tools. That's why this section will become an invaluable resource for you: By examining and gaining an understanding of the strategies used in high-price inspiration rooms, you will learn how to translate what you see to a space that's uniquely yours.

In this section you will discover what tools you should have in your decorating toolbox. You will find out the basics of balance and scale—and why the relationship between furnishings and decorative elements must be in harmony to stand the test of time. You will see how contrast—in color, texture, and shape—can make a room go from blah to beautiful and why it's important to establish a clear focal point in any space. And you will learn the ropes of mixing and matching patterns and treasures you've collected throughout your lifetime. In all you will gain a better understanding of ten decorating and design strategies that will guide you while you decorate any room in your home.

Along the way you will also be treated to additional information on everything from establishing a pleasing lighting scheme and successfully bringing natural elements indoors to how to re-create some of the very best projects featured on *Sensible Chic*. And, as an added bonus, each room has a special *Look for Less* section, dedicated to giving you budget-savvy solutions for achieving a high-end look.

SECTION 2:
Know Your Style
Stylish interiors can take many forms, but when you are faced with a clean decorating slate—or you are ready to redesign an existing space—it may be difficult to determine the exact look you want to attain. If you are stuck and need a nudge, browse this section to help you choose a

look that's right for you. By examining your personal style, what foods you like, how you enjoy spending time with friends and family—or alone—you will be well on your way to making a space that's an accurate reflection of who you are and what you like.

This section begins with a fun style quiz. By answering the questions you will see where your decorating tendencies lie: traditional, contemporary, ethnic, country/cottage, or chic—five of the most popular styles featured on *Sensible Chic*. After a quick summary of each style, you will have an opportunity to explore each in detail, from the types of furnishings and decorative accessories you should incorporate into your room to the colors and fabrics that best suit the style.

By using tear-outs from an old book and readily available mats and frames, the Sensible Chic team was able to create artwork in an instant. Although the budget-friendly artwork above right doesn't share the same subject matter as the originals above left, the stylized shapes and similar matting and framing make them suitable for a tropical-style space—for more than $1,300 less.

Ethnic decorating below pays homage to the native peoples, crafts, and beliefs of the country of origin. This book explores Asian design, African style, and tropical decor. See page 112 to start your ethnic design journey.

Traditional spaces have a regal appearance, often with priceless antiques and opulent fabrics fit for royalty. The bedroom above is no exception. To find out more about this classic style, turn to page 100.

Rustic furnishings, natural fabrics like cotton and wool, and a nod to the stars and stripes make the bedroom right true-blue country. See page 118 for information on country style.

SECTION 3:
The Ultimate Sensible Shopping Guide

No guide to Sensibly Chic decorating would be complete without a feature on shopping—and this amazing name-your-price shopping section illustrates how easy it is to choose the right elements to decorate your home at whatever price you want to spend.

The section begins with a no-nonsense guide to making a plan and determining a budget. Although thinking about money matters may seem daunting, these key steps will make your next room redo more enjoyable and affordable. The most important thing to remember is you don't have to do everything at once: Good design takes time, and it isn't necessary to pull together all the perfect furnishings and accessories to capture the look you are after in just a day. Look at the living room on page 11; by starting with a few key pieces it is possible to let a space grow over time—and as your resources allow.

Next you will learn how to select the right sofas, case goods, bedding, lighting, and more that will fit your lifestyle and your budget by examining pieces at varying quality and price levels. Along the way you'll gain an understanding of furniture construction techniques, how to determine the size of area rug you

should purchase for any given room, and what to look for in window treatments and more before you buy. You'll feel more confident when you shop—and you'll have the satisfaction of knowing you've made smart decisions.

You will also be treated to an insider shopping guide: From flea markets and tag sales to factory outlets and exclusive merchandise marts, you will discover where the bargains are—and what to look for to ensure you get quality for your dollar. As an added bonus, a complete listing of great resources is provided, beginning on page 186.

Multipurpose Masterpieces

If you live in a small apartment or a home you view as temporary, look for multipurpose furniture that can move with you when you relocate. A simple parsons table, for example, can serve as a desk now and be transformed into a nightstand or dining room buffet later. A wooden garden bench can act as a coffee table today, yet later provide additional seating in a larger living room—or be moved outdoors. The trick is to find pieces with clean, defined lines and enduring style that can easily transition into any decorating style you employ down the road. If the piece won't work as is, paint it, slipcover it, or change the hardware to encourage its new design direction.

SECTION 4:
Sensibly Chic Projects

Whether it's making a pillow from remnants of a luxurious fabric you found for a steal or adding a fresh coat of paint to an old dresser that's been stashed in your attic, there's nothing quite as satisfying as knowing you did the job yourself—and that's what this section is all about. More than a dozen project ideas, complete with step-by-step instructions and estimated completion times, allow you to fashion and embellish furnishings and accessories tailored to your personal style. To help you identify at a glance the project that best

Week after week, Sensible Chic Host Brooke Channon right takes viewers on an exciting decorating adventure.

Jen Jordan, Sensible Chic Design Coordinator, far right develops innovative solutions and creates cost-effective projects to get a high-end look for less.

fits your budget, each project includes an estimated materials cost. Finally, valuable techniques—from painting and staining wood to making window treatments in a snap—are explained, giving you the power to get decorating impact in an instant.

Are You Ready?

Now that you've had an opportunity to see what's waiting for you in the following pages, it's time to start your next decorating adventure the *Sensible Chic* way. During your journey you'll see amazing interiors, and you'll undoubtedly dream about how you want your own home to be. Just remember: What you see on these pages—or on TV—is achievable, and when you are armed with your decorating toolbox, you'll face each new decorating challenge head-on.

A

B

Chair to Compare

Despite having similar shapes and being constructed of like materials (beechwood and chrome), one of these contemporary-style chairs retails for $750; you'll only spend $120 for the other. Can you spot which is which?

A. Hawley & Company $120 B. Dauphin $750

Step One If you are starting with a clean slate similar to this, put your decorating dollars into pieces that promote functionality. The light taupe color and clean lines ensure the sofa can be dressed up or down to look great in a room decorated in any style. The white side tables—that lend themselves to nearly any style—stand in as a makeshift coffee table, and a tall lamp offers just the right amount of light for reading.

Step Two Now it's time to step up the style! A coat of light sage-color paint brings the walls to life. The two white tables now become end tables. Topped with striking lamps with brushed-silver bases and a vase of flowers, the tables make way for a burst of color: two deep eggplant-color, leather-covered ottomans. These versatile pieces offer functional seating, a place to set reading materials, or a spot to rest tired feet. The final addition to this living room in progress is a comfy chair that completes the conversation grouping.

Step Three To finish the room, the floor, windows, and a focal-point wall get their due attention. Deep green panels dress the windows, and an area rug provides a dose of pattern and lively color. The wall treatment—1x3 boards equally spaced between the window and French doors and topped with a plate rail, all painted a sunny yellow—firmly establishes this wall (and the sofa) as the focal point of the room. Tabletop accessories and eggplant-color pillows also give the room a boost.

Sensible Solutions for Decorating Dilemmas: 10 Lessons for Living

Whether you are decorating your first home or your fifth, you have undoubtedly faced myriad challenges. You are not alone: When it comes to a task such as choosing paint colors, questions are bound to arise—and chances are you seek the same answers countless others in your situation do. This section is designed to help you easily tackle ten common decorating dilemmas—from selecting a color scheme and creating a focal point to determining the most functional furniture arrangement for any room in your home. By studying the ten amazing inspiration rooms and their Sensibly Chic counterparts, you will have the confidence to face any decorating challenge.

makeover room $1,712

Lesson One | Wake Up to Scale

When decorating any room, consider the size of an object and its impact on the size of the space it occupies—and the other objects surrounding it. This will help you strike a harmonious balance. In this example creating drama and the illusion of luxury in an uninspired guest bedroom hinges on the interplay between size and scale. Take cues from this exciting Sensible Makeover to establish a similar look for less in any room in your home.

How Do You Want a Room to Feel? Before purchasing a single piece of furniture or painting one wall, envision the mood you want to conjure in a room. In doing so you will lay a solid foundation on which to create a room that looks and feels the way you want it to. Inspiration room designer Val Fiscalini visualized a pampering guest retreat, soothing to both the eyes and touch. The wall color helped set an inviting tone: Cool aqua blue with a hint of green has an immediate calming effect on all who enter.

The aqua color translates easily to the makeover room; however, because of a slanted cathedral ceiling, *Sensible Chic* designer Jen Jordan opted to paint just one wall, not all four. "We didn't want it

	Sensible Makeover	Inspiration
Canopy Bed	$235	$6,000
Bedding	$200	$3,098
Pillows/Bolster	$230	$1,195
Window Treatments	$70	$9,700
Dream Artwork	$50	$150
Side Tables/ Accessories	$528	$7,916
Upholstered Bench	$125	$2,000
Wall Sconces	$75	$3,600
Wall Paint	$70	$100
Wall Art	$84	$3,200
Floor Coverings	$45	$2,100
TOTAL	$1,712	$39,059

Dreaming a little dream is just as easy in the Sensible Makeover bedroom left as it is in the significantly more expensive inspiration room right. A cool color scheme of blue and taupe sets a relaxing tone in both spaces, while beautifully detailed furnishings and accessories—in just the right scale and proportion for the rooms—pull the look together.

inspiration room $39,059

By painting only one wall, this bedroom has one commanding focal point: the bed and the serene "dream" artwork. A pile of plump pillows in soothing colors and luxurious fabrics adds a pampering touch to the room's feature attraction.

to feel like a fishbowl," she explains. The larger the surface, the more imposing the color may be and the more difficult it is to reach high spaces. In this case leaving some walls cream in color made the task of painting more manageable—yet the effect is just as alluring. And besides being a smart use of time and resources, painting only the wall behind the bed puts the focus where it should be: on the bed and the custom artwork.

How Much Furniture Do You Need in the Room?
Sometimes less is more, especially in a guest bedroom, where dressers and drawer space are not as essential as they are in a master bedroom. The more elements there are, the more space they occupy, and the greater the need to keep furnishings small.

In this case fewer pieces of furniture allow latitude to play with the size. In the inspiration room a curvaceous $6,000 canopy bed reaches high to the ceiling, stating its obvious importance. Adjacent his-and-her nightstands echo the tone with similar smooth lines, adding interest on either side of the bed.

"Good design is not all about height and width," Jen says. "It's about weight and substance." If a piece is heavy and chunky, it looks bigger—and potentially out of place in a small room. In the Sensible Makeover room, the canopy bed may have been too cumbersome had Jen not removed an ornate headboard and footboard and replaced them with painted 2x2 wood strips. This not only lightened the impressions of an otherwise large-scale furnishing, but it also helped achieve a look that closely mirrored the commanding focal point in

the inspiration room. Topping the posts with painted gold finials adds touches of extravagant detail—at a much more palatable cost of $235.

Use Color and Texture to Continue the Theme
In a small room use light colors to visually expand the space. Although the canopy bed is black, the linens and window treatments offset the weight with their serene neutral tones. "You can play a lot of visual tricks,"

Jen says, "to make a room look grand."

Starting with the bed as a focal point, the inspiration room linens are perfectly pampering. A silk and linen damask duvet cover, a chintz linen bed skirt, and an oversize bolster create dimension with their subtle stripes and textures—but how does one translate them to affordable comfort and style?

Jen suggests looking for visual softness. Although the faux suede used for the duvet

SENSIBLE PROJECT
Art with a Message

Custom artwork is a breeze to make with store-bought canvas, vinyl letters, and common paint supplies. Use this technique to make your own statement, such as a child's name or a word or phrase that sets a mood you want to create in a room.

ONE: Position the vinyl letters on the canvas. Peel away the backing material.

TWO: Mix 4 parts glaze with 1 part paint. Apply the mixture to the canvas in a swirling or dabbing motion with a brush or lint-free rag to create a mottled, textural appearance; let dry.

THREE: Peel the letters off the canvas to reveal the word or phrase.

Painted black accents on the votive candleholder and trinket box right connect them to the rest of the room for little expense or effort. The shapely style of the table on which these accents stand is compatible with the simple lines of the other furniture pieces in the room.

cover in the Sensible Makeover room may not be as crisp (or expensive) as linen, it clearly adds a luxurious feel, distinguished from everyday flat cotton. "I like beauty with function," Jen adds. Besides accomplishing a lavish look, faux suede offers a machine-washable advantage, making the fabric more practical for everyday living.

Another interplay of color and texture that sets the tone in the room is the "dream" artwork. The subtle message in both rooms has a background of mottled blue and white and white lettering. The only discernable difference between the two pieces is the price: The artwork in the inspiration room cost $150, while Jen created her own version for a mere $50.

Use Window Tricks Just as you can create drama and visual interest with furnishings, you can also use size and scale to manipulate the view. To make a room appear taller and more elegant, hang window treatments high on the wall, above the window frame, as was done in the inspiration room. This visual trick heightens the space, and longer panels have a richer, more customized look. Because the

Sensible Makeover room has a high ceiling, the panels are hung just above the window frame, allowing the long panels to puddle on the floor. This adds to the sophisticated look. The trim at the top, which coordinates with the duvet cover, contributes contrast and detail

▶ For a video demonstration of the table transformation *above*, visit HGTV.com/sensiblechic

without being too fussy. This subtle splash of color adds punch to the light-color panels. Using quick embellishment tricks like this allows you to coordinate a plain panel with other elements in the room.

If you are looking for a stylish way to hang any type of window treatment—not just traditional panels—Jen recommends curtain ring clips, which are available at home centers. "Theoretically you can hang up sheets," she says. "You're not limited to buying panels off the shelf."

Add Accents Size and scale are just as important when adding accent furnishings and bedding. To replicate the masculine bedside—grounded by a rich, fluted dark table that cost a whopping $4,370 with accessories—Jen focused on size and shape. She adapted a simple console-style table she found by adding dentil detail for visual interest and painting the entire piece dark brown. Continuing the exotic

theme on the tabletop, Jen chose a stone sculpture based on its small scale and tranquil suggestion. In total the Sensible Makeover table was produced for a mere $170.

For the room's feminine side, Jen looked for something that would mirror the custom silver-finish table of the inspiration room. To do so she removed the spherical center of a brass table, painted and antiqued the base in a silver color, then embellished the glass top with transparent scrapbooking pebbles for a distinctive look. "I could have stenciled a dotted rim or stamped little circles in silver paint," Jen explains. An open mind, she says, is key to reinventing

Sensible Shopping Tip

For a luxury look in linens, choose a thread count of at least 250 threads per inch. The higher the thread count, the better the quality. See page 140 for more information on selecting bedding.

a luxury look for less. In this case she was able to create a similar look at a fraction of the cost: The inspiration room table and accessories cost $3,350, while Jen's version came to just $360.

The $2,000 silk-upholstered bench also helps create depth in the inspiration room. Jen pulled off a similar look for just $125 by painting a padded piano bench and covering it with pale celery damask fabric. The added benefit of the less expensive version is storage inside, which provides space for clothes, blankets, and linens.

Finally pillows of various shapes and

In replicating the Buddha art in the inspiration room, Jen says the scale and Asian-inspired design *far left* were more important than a larger, chunkier (and more expensive) piece.

Fabric-covered foam, embellished with ribbon and button details *left*, looks as authentic as a designer bolster. For the Sensible Makeover room, Jen glued two 36-inch lengths of foam together to create the extralong cushion—an economical way to get a custom look.

Pillow Talk

Pillows are more than functional: They are all about making a comfortable design statement. Follow these cues when you purchase or make pillows for your bedroom:

- **Modify pillow sizes and shapes depending on the style.** For a modern look, use fewer pillows in similar square or rectangular shapes. Keep the height low and avoid circles.

- **Create a feeling of luxury, using lots of pillows** in contrasting shapes and textures. Large square forms called Euro shams (26"x26") add height—and drama—at the head of the bed.

- **Stack pillows of different sizes** in front of each other to create a sense of fullness. The more traditional or country style you want, the more pillows you can use.

sizes add visual interest and comfort to the bed. In the inspiration room the custom pillows made of silk and linen were created for $1,195. For $230 a similar statement is made with a striking bolster embellished with ribbons and buttons and ready-made pillow shams with a tone-on-tone diamond motif.

See the Light When looking to replicate the sconces for the makeover room, Jen says, "You have to decide which elements are most important." None of the sconces she found matched the ornate silhouette and detail of the inspiration room originals, so she opted for simpler variations. "They ideally would have been more ornate," she explains, "but the scale of these fixtures fit the room better."

In both rooms artwork between the sconces and side tables completes a line from floor to ceiling, enhancing the overall visual impact and making the walls look wide and embracing.

The wall sconces in the inspiration room were difficult to replicate because of their three-arm design, electric hookup, and unusual scale. However, the flea market find below is a great alternative: The design is more modest, but the sconces still have a strong presence on the walls, as is evidenced left.

The Look for Less

Use these cues, inspired by this amazing guest room makeover, to design and decorate any room so that it looks and feels as expensive as a designer original.

▶ **If you're intimidated by painting a whole room, simplify the job** by adding color to one accent wall. This saves time and money and allows one wall to become an immediate focal point.

▶ **When shopping for furniture, imagine pieces without the detail.** Look for parts that you can easily disassemble, so you can adapt them to your style. In the Sensible Makeover this trick was used for both the bed, which originally had an ornate headboard and footboard, and the feminine side table, which had a large sphere in its base.

▶ **Save money by mixing and matching.** To get a personalized look, search for complementary colors and textures that aren't necessarily sold in a coordinated set. In the makeover room the bedding and pillows were pieced together: a duvet cover found on a clearance table and a bolster pillow made from two pieces of foam and covered with inexpensive fabric and ribbon trim. The plain window treatments are trimmed with fabric that complements the duvet cover and ribbon trim on the pillow, so all the elements look like part of the "set."

▶ **Artwork doesn't need to be expensive.** Tear-outs from old botanical books and insect guides, postcards, and advertisements are great examples of inexpensive art, as the eye-catching pieces in the Sensible Makeover room prove. Look for these items at flea markets, garage sales, and estate sales and surround them with ready-cut mats and discount store frames for thrifty artwork in minutes.

makeover room $2,290

Lesson Two | A Toast to Balance

Whether a room design is symmetrical (aligned equally along a central axis), asymmetrical (less formal with variation in shapes, colors, and patterns), or radial (starting from a central point and moving outward), balance is key to making it feel right. Reminiscent of a rustic Tuscan farmhouse, this makeover models a pleasing balance of casual form, warm lighting, and natural textures. Use the ideas on the following pages as inspiration to bring balance to any room in your home.

Establish a Focal Point When planning a layout for any room, start by choosing a piece of furniture, an accessory, or an architectural element that serves as the center of attention. This focal point sets the tone for the size, visual weight, and shape of the other elements in the room. In the case of this Sensible Makeover, the armoire already existed in the empty hallway.

Slatted doors lighten the visual weight, but the overall look is large and heavy, suggesting that heavy furnishings—such as a hefty table—are required to balance the focal-point armoire.

Although the inspiration room didn't have a large freestanding piece like the armoire, the large table is a commanding focal point in its own right. According

	Sensible Makeover	Inspiration
Candelier	$125	$650
Farmhouse Table	$250	$6,000
Dining Chairs	$600	$17,760
Riddling Racks	$550	$1,000
Ladder/Wine Safe	$250	$6,150
French Tapestry	$100	$15,000
Artwork	$150	$3,600
Wall Sconces	$32	$500
Tabletop Accessories	$55	$2,110
Stemware/Dishware	$118	$1,321
Wall Treatment	$60	$3,000
TOTAL	$2,290	$57,091

An unused foyer with little natural light becomes an intimate venue for socialites and wine lovers left. The only symmetrical grouping in the room is the artwork and neighboring wall sconces (shown on page 25); other randomly placed elements establish a casual tone. The makeover is a striking resemblance to the much costlier antiques-filled wine cellar dining room right.

inspiration room $57,091

A tall antique armoire with slatted doors—the only pre-existing item in the once-desolate hallway—hails from Mexico and lends itself to a rustic farmhouse feel. It is an ideal place to stash dishware and serving pieces when the room is not in use.

to inspiration room designer Joseph Hittinger, "We looked for a piece with modest heft to ground the room." That antique table cost a whopping $6,000, nearly three times the cost of the entire Sensible Makeover space! The makeover table, purchased for $250, is similar in weight to the original but lacks the carved grape detail on the more expensive example. "We decided it was fine to use a plain table with the same structure," *Sensible Chic*'s Jen Jordan explains. With its deep wood tones, this table still has an aged, rustic feel that suits the style of the room.

To complement the antique table in the inspiration room, large dining chairs were introduced. The dark-stained, finely turned arms and legs of the chairs are attractive details, and the tapestry upholstery is a softening feature, but each chair cost nearly $3,000—so the task was to find chairs that were equally attractive but significantly less expensive. Jen found four matching side chairs also with delicately turned legs and upholstered in European-style fabric.

She added two chairs in solid-color fabrics on the ends of the table to achieve a similar look and provide a pleasing symmetry around the oversize table. Although all the chairs are very different from the originals, they still have a centuries-old look and feel.

Weigh the Walls Adding visual interest around the perimeter of a room—using paint, artwork, and items of varying heights—often eases the visual load, especially if oversize furnishings dominate the center of the floor. In the spirit of the inspiration room, Jen enriched the existing cream-color walls with a wash of sand-color paint, glaze, and water to make the surface appear old and worn. This textural effect sets the stage for the old-world appeal, yet was

A print, which features subject matter similar to the artwork in the inspiration room, and sconces made of a stonelike material above offer visual relief from all the large, heavy objects in the room.

Design Detail

Visual weight—whether an object appears heavy or light—is important in achieving balance. Large objects, bright patterns, warm colors, and rough textures are visually heavy, while small objects, cool colors, and smooth surfaces appear lighter.

The chairs were purchased upholstered, but slipcovers can achieve a comparable look. The nailhead tack details left provide old-world appeal that complements the overall feel of the room.

The tapered cherry shelf right is similar in shape and function to the antique Indonesian ladder featured in the inspiration room. Branches placed in a large pot nearby add an inexpensive organic touch in an instant.

Riddling racks, once used for fermenting champagne, are reinvented as wine racks, uncorking conversation while adding texture against the wall below. The large pieces are in just the right scale to work in this long, narrow room and strike a nice balance between the other furnishings and accessories in the room.

much less costly to create than the exposed brick treatment in the inspiration room.

Realizing that the riddling racks (used for fermenting champagne) are critical to the integrity of the makeover room, Jen followed the inspiration room's lead and purchased the same pieces from a French antiques dealer in San Francisco. "There are some things you just can't compromise," she says. The racks not only anchor the wine tasting theme by serving an important function, but they also add dimension and texture to the flat walls.

To balance the racks in the inspiration

room, a tall antique Indonesian ladder and low-standing antique vault draw the eye to opposing levels, while both offer additional storage and display space. Because replicating these pieces would be cost-prohibitive in the Sensible Makeover room, Jen looked for less expensive alternatives. A contemporary cherry unit with tapered shelves is an adequate substitute for the ladder, while an inexpensive wire rack suffices for the vault when treated with a special rusting agent. "The metal provides contrast against the wood pieces," Jen explains. Besides being functional these two pieces create textural balance.

Use Artistic Sense Especially in a room that's intended to be casual, elements need not be formally aligned. Because store-bought tapestries similar to the one in the inspiration room were either too bold or too expensive, Jen made her own tapestry from an inexpensive fabric remnant. She hemmed the top and bottom seams and left raw edges on the sides to make the tapestry look old and worn—the perfect balance between soft and unrefined.

In the inspiration room an expensive oil painting depicting a woman with a basket of fruit serves as a focal point on the wall adjacent to the riddling racks. In the Sensible Makeover room a much less expensive piece of art—a flea market reproduction of a merriment scene similar to the original—finds a home on the wall opposite the riddling racks. This wall—with the artwork, two sconces, and the tall cherry shelf—is a pleasing counterpoint to the visually heavy racks.

Add Visual Interest Visually lighter objects give the eye relief against weighty furniture in any room. "We realized we needed nice ambient lighting to add that

A ceramic bowl full of fruits and vegetables right adds a burst of color—and an invitation to merriment—to the table in the inspiration room.

SENSIBLE PROJECT
Custom Candelier

If you desire a sense of drama and a hint of old-world ambience in any room in your home, this is the project for you.

ONE: Cut a piece of ¼-inch plywood into a square or rectangle of the desired size. Measure and mark a center square or rectangle, approximately 9 inches from the edges of the plywood. Cut out the center shape.

TWO: Drill a hole in each of the four corners of the plywood platform; secure an eyehook into each hole with a nut.

THREE: To give the plywood an aged appearance, spray-paint the top, bottom, and sides with copper-color, brass-color, or black paint. Feel free to mix colors and apply the paint in an uneven fashion for an authentic aged look.

FOUR: Attach four lengths of chain to the platform (one piece to each eyehook) so that the platform will hang approximately 7 feet above the floor (30 inches above a dining table). Attach the chains to a heavy-duty hook in the ceiling.

FIVE: Arrange small glass or metal trays on the platform and set candles of various heights, widths, and colors on the trays. **Caution:** Do not leave burning candles unattended.

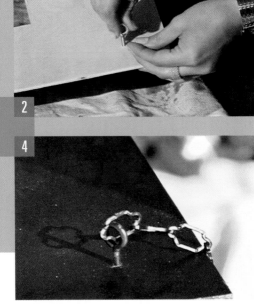

▶ For a video demonstration of the candelier project, visit HGTV.com/sensiblechic

final dimension," says Joseph Hittinger of the inspiration room. Different sizes and numbers of candles can be lit depending on the mood and desired amount of light. A brighter light source was not important, Joseph explains, because the goal was to create a comfortable coziness.

For the makeover room, the solution was an inexpensive custom candelier that centered candlelight directly over the table. Instead of welding metal as in the original piece, the *Sensible Chic* team painted and aged a wooden platform to look like metal, then hung it with chains from the ceiling. Flat, inconspicuous glass trays protect the surface when the candles are lit, preventing wax from dripping onto the tabletop.

Companion wall sconces on either side of the painting in both rooms also introduce ambient lighting and visual texture. Because the fruit-embossed inspiration room pieces were difficult to replicate, Jen searched for something else that would be appropriate for the style of the room. "There was a lot more texture in the inspiration room, so we brought it into the sconces," she says. Her choice of stonelike fixtures added old-world detail for a total of $32—a far cry from the $500 spent on the two sconces in

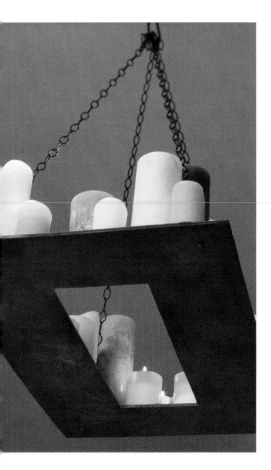

Mismatched candles are grouped on top of a painted wood platform that is suspended from chains and hangs from the ceiling. When the candles are lit, the flickering light casts a warm glow perfect for intimate gatherings in this dining area.

the inspiration room. Although the artwork and sconces in the makeover room aren't nearly as costly as those in the inspiration room, they still offer a good sense of balance.

Finally, even a connoisseur might mistake the tableware in the less expensive makeover room for authentic because of its earthly colors and mismatched style. Warm amber—instead of clear— glassware and white ceramic and faux pewter dishes were a fraction of the cost of the original antiques, yet they still say "rustic and relaxed."

The Look for Less

Do you desire a room that looks high-priced but is created with inexpensive elements that capture the same ambience? Use these tips to turn any room in your home into a Sensibly Chic space.

▶ **Scope flea markets and garage sales for deals on mismatched chairs that vary in style, size, and decorative elements.** This approach is perfect when you want to achieve a relaxed, informal feel.

▶ **Use your imagination when shopping for accessories.** If the finish is not right but the price is, think about how it can be manipulated—for instance repainted or given a metal leaf finish. In this makeover room an ordinary wine rack was given old-world charm with a coat of metal-look spray paint.

▶ **If original artwork is a budget buster, consider poster art.** If you desire an aged look that would be appropriate in an old-world or rustic setting, "doctor" the image to make it look authentic. Mount the poster onto canvas using spray adhesive; then add dimension with a coat of modeling paste or acrylic varnish, following the manufacturer's instructions.

▶ **Whether used for a candelier, a display in an empty firebox, or for a tabletop arrangement, consider unmatched candle sets.** Mismatched single candles are not only less expensive, but they're also more interesting in a grouping than too-similar candles.

▶ **Slipcovers—ready-made or custom-made—offer unlimited decorating potential.** You can change the look of any seating piece for the season or for a special event. This also allows you to cover a furnishing with worn upholstery or purchase a more expensive piece that can be re-covered for years to come for decorating longevity. And you can embellish any slipcover with ties, trim, or beads to dress it up.

makeover room $2,854

Lesson Three Color Me Modern

Color—from warm reds to cool blues and everything between—has the ability to affect our moods and attitudes. Our personalities are reflected through color in the clothes we wear and the cars we drive. And, when it comes to decorating our homes, color often goes hand in hand with the style we want to achieve to set just the right tone. If you desire a space that's styled with rich color and contemporary comfort, use this Sensible Makeover to jump-start your room redo.

	Sensible Makeover	Inspiration
Sofa(s)	$1,200	$10,000
Cowboy Art	$80	$1,000
Standing Screen	$150	$5,700
Carpet/Area Rug	$228	$2,300
Ottoman/Accessories	$345	$2,285
Pillows	$196	$2,100
Media Cabinet	$100	$4,420
Stuffed Chair/Side Table	$409	$2,420
Glassware/Ceramics	$46	$12,820
Wall Treatment	$100	$2,000
TOTAL	$2,854	$45,045

Choose a Color Palette Whether contemporary or traditional, the colors and patterns you choose for a room work together to build its character. In the case of the inspiration room, tie-dyed orange and cinnamon rings on a sofa pillow inspired the palette. Beginning with the walls, designers Jo Ann Hartley and Jennifer Hershon chose to upholster the room in rust-color fabric with a subdued geometric pattern, which introduces texture and absorbs sound. This was an important consideration in a room designed for watching movies and listening to music—all the while enveloping the room in warm color.

The *Sensible Chic* team took its cues from the color to achieve a similar look, yet stayed within the budget. "We chose to pick up a similar color in paint,"

Comfortable seating for television viewing, conversing, and casual snacking are priorities in a media room, where people tend to gather to watch a movie and mingle. A bold red on the walls sets the stage for contemporary comfort in both the makeover room left and the inspiration room right; the style is also evident in the low-lying furnishings and a thoughtful mix of straight-line and curvilinear shapes.

inspiration room $45,045

The Power of Color

Close your eyes and imagine walking into a room with bright red walls. How do you feel? Invigorated and energized or calm and mellow? Now imagine that same room bathed in soft baby blue. How do you feel now? Chances are you would feel different in each space, due in part to how you responded to your surroundings on an emotional level.

In general, warm colors—red, orange, and yellow—are happy, lively colors that impart a feeling of energy and action. Conversely, cool colors—blue, green, and violet—tend to relax and restore the spirit. And, let's not forget about versatile neutrals—white, black, and all shades of brown—that have the ability to blend into the background when paired with cool or warm colors or quietly and calmly take center stage when varying shades of white or brown are combined in one space.

When choosing a color scheme for any room, keep in mind that often the most successful color schemes are a combination of cool and warm colors, with a dash of neutral thrown in to either punctuate or tone down the dominant hues.

Most often a particular color scheme works well with a given style: Soft pastels and whites are perfect for a cottage-style space, while spicy oranges and reds are just right for an exotic look. However, while design rules can certainly dictate a given style, *Sensible Chic*'s Jen Jordan says rules should not infringe on your personal taste. "If you love yellow," she says, "that's fine. Build a new color palette around yellow to make it modern," if you desire a contemporary look. She adds, "When it's something surrounding you, it should be something that makes you happy."

style will change the look and the tone. For instance, a Windsor chair painted in a bright fuchsia hue will look great in a contemporary dining space, but give the same chair a distressed paint finish in white and it will be best suited for country decor.

Use Shapes to Define the Look Shapes—squares, rectangles, triangles, and circles—and lines—straight, smooth, and curving—of the various elements in a room also contribute to the mood and attitude it exudes. It's often the mix of these shapes and lines that makes a room interesting. The inspiration room designers chose a sleek wraparound sectional covered in faux suede and an oversize leather ottoman, both of which offer plush, comfortable seating. Steering away from expensive custom pieces, Jen found a comparable love seat and sofa with simple lines that were covered in less costly faux suede upholstery. A big square ottoman, tan instead of raspberry, and purchased for $300 at a consignment shop, complements the color scheme and becomes the center of conversation—for $1,500 less!

Wraparound arms on a custom-made club chair, which is on casters to make it mobile, also define the modern look in the inspiration room. Jen opted for a slightly smaller chair. "Everything we were finding made a different statement," Jen says of the makeover room. With exposed legs, a curved back, and simple lines, the chair—covered in soft tan leather—still

▶ For a video demonstration of the wall screen project *opposite*, visit HGTV.com/sensiblechic

Sensible Chic designer Jen Jordan explains. "The rich color was enough."

Jen says stronger hues are typically associated with a contemporary style, but people are changing the rules about color. "If you like neutrals or pastels," she says, "it's OK to use whatever you like. Simple lines [for the furnishings and accessories] are most important." She explains that the same color in different contexts can look very different—just as changing the color of a furnishing can alter its look. Furnishings and accents of a different

A sofa and love seat purchased for the makeover room are affordable compromises to the expensive sectional, which is showcased in the inspiration room. The color of the two pieces blends effortlessly with the walls and the other furnishings and still offers ample seating for a group.

To maximize space in a small room, the ottoman doubles as both a coffee table and a footrest *right*. The media cabinet against the wall is an inexpensive sideboard with the legs removed—and it is a deadringer for the original at $4,320 less.

Design Tip

Balance low-lying objects, such as low-profile sofas, chairs, and coffee tables, with tall furniture or accents, such as a piece of art, an armoire, or a large plant.

contributes to the contemporary feel of the room.

Finally, the inspiration room designer used nesting end tables with a dark stained finish. A perfect match for classic modern style with their tall rectangular shapes and curvilinear corners, these tables were also practical, occupying minimum floor space when nested, yet delivering on demand when needed to hold beverages. Because it was impossible to find comparable pieces for the makeover room, the *Sensible Chic* team decided to purchase the very same tables. A splurge

indeed, but because these pieces are so versatile and add to the overall look of the room, it was well worth the cost.

Repeat the Motif A visually balanced room relies on recurring elements; in the inspiration room the stage was set with repeating geometric designs in red and gold on the wall-to-wall carpeting. In the makeover space, to keep costs in line, Jen opted for a smaller area rug with a comparable geometric design. Placing it in the middle of the conversation area anchors it as a key design element. The

rug has another important function: It pulls together all the colors in the room, from the red on the walls to the tan of the ottoman, and even ushers in pleasing contrast with cool greens.

The wall screens in both rooms echo the carpet and rug patterns in a series of repeating squares. Besides adding eye-level interest in the corner of both spaces, they also add height where nearly everything else sits low. The original screen made of wood and brushed nickel cost $5,700— far more than the *Sensible Chic* team could afford. Jen duplicated the pricey original

Nesting side tables right—the essence of a clean-line modern look—are the same in this room as the inspiration room. Their rectangular shape justify the additional cost, and—as an added bonus—they tie in with the pattern of the rug.

using plywood, dowels, and metallic paint. "Our screen is a little chunkier," she admits, but with a price difference of $5,550 it's a trade-off worth making. She adds that a plain black or espresso-color three-panel screen would speak just as strongly to the room's clean look.

The rectangular shape is repeated yet again in the audiovisual cabinet placed beneath the screen on the focal point wall. Standing low to the ground and made of mahogany and copper, the $4,420 inspiration room piece provides valuable media storage as well as a diversion from the stark white movie screen. In the makeover room existing wall units— additional rectangular shapes—limited the size and scope of the cabinet, but the *Sensible Chic* team was able to come up with a remarkably similar look—for only $100. "We decided to go with a value option," Jen explains. She removed the legs from a store-bought sideboard, painted it chocolate brown, and affixed a row of vertical half-round molding strips to the front. A finishing coat of metallic copper paint completes the decorative facade.

Accessorize with Finesse

When decorating a room, well-planned accessories can make a big impression. The artwork on the wall in the inspiration room (another grouping of square and rectangular shapes) plays into the home theater theme with black and white images of well-known American cowboy actors. Jen used comparable movie photos, but says that any images would work as long as they're displayed in a modern way: evenly spaced in a continuous mat. Although the custom piece in the inspiration room is large and spans a good deal of the wall behind the sectional, the makeover version is shorter; however, it still is right in scale above the smaller sofa.

Zebra-inspired vases and colored glassware are other eye-catching additions. With simple geometric lines and compatible colors, they reflect the contemporary style of both rooms. The black and white vases connect to the white movie screen in the high-cost room while providing contrast against the rust-color walls. For the Sensible

Contemporary Clues

A modern look is sleek and clean. To capture the essence of this style, look for these elements (see page 106 for more information on this style):

- **Simple lines.** Look for geometric shapes, such as squares, rectangles, and circles, as opposed to traditional-style swanlike curves. Avoid dramatic, extravagant detail: Romance does not belong in a modern room. The purer the shape, the more contemporary it is.

- **Tailored designs.** Furniture typically is close to the floor with exposed legs and feet and has form-fitting upholstery. Avoid skirts, pleating, and tucking of any form.

- **Bold color.** Typically, modern is defined by neutrals and shots of bold color; however, Jen stresses that the rules are changing. What feeling do you want to convey? Choose a color that you love, then design a modern room around it, tying it to the space through carefully selected furnishings and accessories.

SENSIBLE PROJECT
Cool Ceramics

The beauty of expensive handmade pottery can be yours in an instant! Just purchase ceramic vessels with interesting shapes, low-tack painter's tape, and spray paint to create a custom look.

ONE: Paint the vessel white, using spray paint that's specially formulated for ceramic surfaces; let dry.

TWO: Adhere low-tack tape to the surface of the vessel. You can create random zebralike stripes similar to the piece shown in the makeover room or uniform stripes for a formal look. Ensure the edges of the tape are firmly adhered to the surface (so paint doesn't seep underneath).

THREE: Paint the vessel black with one thin, even coat, again using spray paint that's formulated for ceramic surfaces. Immediately remove the tape; let dry.

Makeover Jen re-created the inspiration room vases by spray-painting abstract ceramic forms white, then over-spraying nonsymmetrical lines in black. The result is simply stunning—on a budget.

Finally, a collection of oversize floor pillows invites a roomful of guests to recline. "These are great ways to add extra seating to your room without adding much to the budget," Jen explains. While plush custom pillows with rounded edges are featured in the inspiration room, store-bought cushions continue the modern geometric theme in the makeover room. In both rooms pillows on the sofas tie in with the colors and add visual interest in a focused space. For a custom touch in the makeover room, the rectangular faux pony-fur pillow complements the cowboy pictures on the wall.

"If you have something white," Jen says, such as the flat-panel television screen, "add a few other white pieces to blend it together." Zebra-inspired vases opposite top provide stark contrast against the rich warm and neutral hues throughout the space.

Look for inexpensive art, such as handblown Mexican glass, that an artisan could have made. The yellow and red pieces above echo the bold tones and geometric shapes in the Sensibly Chic room.

Design Tip

Display the things you love in ways that tie into the theme of your room. Instead of the cowboy photos, for instance, theater playbills could work just as well in this setting. As a general rule, the larger the frame around the image, the more contemporary the look. Visit art supply and crafts stores for a multitude of inexpensive mat and frame options to showcase your favorite pieces.

The Look for Less

Getting an expensive custom-designed look in your home for less may be easier than you think! Use these tools to assist with your next room redo:

▶ **Substitute paint for fabric on walls.** In this room Jen used a rust-red paint instead of expensive upholstery to introduce color on the walls. If you desire visual texture that more closely resembles fabric, mix the paint with a glazing medium (1 part paint to 4 parts glaze) and apply with a brush or rag.

▶ **Furnishings with high-quality upholstery offer an almost limitless range of pattern options;** however, if you find a less expensive piece in a similar size and shape but in a solid color, dress it up with pillows or other accents that mimic the more costly original. Such was the case in these rooms: The inspiration room featured a comfy chair covered in a circle-print fabric just right for the contemporary feel, while a less expensive chair—with similar lines but covered in tan leather—in the makeover room is dressed up with a soft chenille throw for a splash of color.

▶ **Instead of expensive wall-to-wall carpeting, smaller decorative area rugs offer equal effectiveness**—and are much less costly. And, if you can't afford a single large rug, layer two or three rugs of a complementary size, color, and pattern.

▶ **Modify store-bought or hand-me-down furniture by removing legs, painting parts, and adding embellishments.** Jen completely changed the look of the audiovisual cabinet by removing its legs, adding half-round moldings, and painting it.

▶ **Inexpensive pillows, decorative throws, and accessories add richness, color, and interest for a minimum investment**—especially if you can incorporate items you already have and love into your redecorated space.

makeover room $3,259

Lesson Four | Mixing and Matching

Creating a space that's distinctly yours is as easy as blending old and new elements in a variety of colors and textures. Although many of the unusual effects in the inspiration room may be imports from far away, the design lessons they teach are close to home: Decorate with the things you love and appreciate diversity. As shown in the budget-savvy, life-size scrapbook, mixing and matching all sorts of styles can create a sophisticated, well-traveled look—without the expense of world travel. Even if you prefer a different decorating style, such as traditional or contemporary, the basics of mixing and matching that you'll learn on the following pages still apply.

Map the Journey When decorating a room of any style, it is important to start with a plan: decide how you will use the room and envision how you want the room to feel. The first consideration? Color: It can set a mood and capture the feeling of any time in history or any location across the globe.

For an exotic-style room such as this, *Sensible Chic*'s Jen Jordan advises choosing a color palette of five or six shades. Paint sample cards from a home center or paint store will provide countless options. Take a selection of cards home, cut them apart, and group the colors to determine

	Sensible Makeover	Inspiration
Wall Paint	$100	$240
Area Rug	$250	$15,500
Window Treatments	$390	$7,000
Chandelier	$260	$6,500
Sofa	$700	$5,000
Pillows	$120	$1,800
Coffee Table	$250	$2,995
Tabletop Accessories	$220	$3,015
Mantel Accessories	$155	$8,700
Side Chairs	$500	$13,000
Suitcases	$139	$2,375
Asian Prints/Trunk	$100	$7,750
Ming-Style Camel/ Sea-Grass Elephant	$75	$2,825
TOTAL	$3,259	$76,700

inspiration room $76,700

Expensive antiques and one-of-a-kind pieces contribute to the exotic elegance of the inspiration room left. By combining items the homeowner already had and thrifty replicas of the unique pieces in the expensive original, the Sensible Makeover opposite proves that great design doesn't have to cost a lot of money.

Bring Nature Indoors

To enhance any decor, take advantage of nature's countless colors, textures, and shapes, following these tips:

- **Real plants are almost always better than silk,** and most are surprisingly easy to maintain. Keep plants in their original pots, cover them with moss, and care for them individually.

- **Planters, pots, and baskets blend best in organic colors,** such as brown, smoky green, and earth tones. Look for containers made of natural materials, including stone, concrete, and terra-cotta, instead of highly finished designer receptacles.

- **Observing plants in their natural habitats,** exploring gardening books, and visiting your local nursery will give you tips on compatible flora and their care.

- **Plant varieties and variation in heights help arrangements look organic and natural**—not contrived.

- **Natural fragrances can add dimension to your decorating.** *Sensible Chic*'s Jen Jordan says candles and potpourri should smell like a lavender field in France, not like a candy store. Look for essential oils, such as bergamot, rosemary, verbena, and lemongrass; avoid sweet, fruity smells.

a pleasing palette. Use your favorites as guidelines when shopping for other pieces in the room. If you already have an inspiration piece, however, you may use it as a springboard for the color palette. In the inspiration room a rare hand-knotted Turkish Oushak rug set the tone. A similar not-so-rare—but just as visually exciting—Oriental rug directed Jen toward a palette of red, green, gold, and khaki with shots of black and blue in the Sensible Makeover space.

Khaki paint on the walls offsets the busy pattern on the floor, adding warmth and sophistication. "The walls lend themselves to an overlay of colors," Jen says. "They're neutral enough that you can change accessories and completely alter the look." This smart approach can be used for rooms decorated in any style: Start with a neutral on the walls, and mix and match furnishings and accessories of different colors as the mood strikes.

Store-bought cotton window panels in a khaki color aren't as lavish as the Indian silk draperies with embroidered red silk bands that hung in the inspiration room. However, the *Sensible Chic* team contrived a way for the panels to work by adding red satin trim along the tops and edges. Embroidered bees on the trim add some detail in the spirit of the original fabric—and the red offers a warm shot of color against the neutral-color panels. This quick trick can enliven any window treatment; if you don't sew, use fusible hem tape for quick and easy customization.

The arrangement right adds a touch of the outdoors to the exotic-style space. All the plants remain in their original pots for ease of care; a covering of moss conceals the pots.

Pack in Comfort When planning furniture for a "well-traveled" room—or any room that will be used for lounging and conversation—comfort is just as important as style. "It's nice if you can afford extra details, but there's nothing wrong with simple," Jen says. At $5,000, the original plush, tufted-back sofa was too expensive for this makeover budget, so Jen decided to forego the buttons. The khaki-color sofa she chose instead stands up to this and any other style because of its simple lines—and at only $700 it is a relative bargain.

Color and texture in the sofa pillows add to the eclectic appeal. "These anchors establish the room as global," Jen explains. Different fabrics—olive velvet, kilim (a woven fabric of Turkish origin), and red satin—suggest a multicultural influence, while reinforcing the earthly color palette. By mixing

pillow fabrics of various textures, patterns, and colors, the neutral-color sofa gains immediate focal-point status.

The coffee table speaks to yet another part of the world with its Asian-influenced curved legs and dark wood. Inspiration room designers Sharon Daroca and Eleanore

Wood-framed armchairs with ribbed chenille upholstery below add natural textures into the mix. The antique trunk and suitcase stack up to the travel theme, inviting drinks and worldly conversation.

Table Tricks

To ensure beverages and books are within easy reach, side tables should stand slightly lower than the arms of the chair they complement. If you can't find the exact table you desire for your room, invent tables of your own from ethnic drums, pedestals, antique boxes, trunks, crocks, or old barrels.

With their placement high on the wall, exotic-theme prints above the homeowner's Florentine chest left balance the space on the other side of the fireplace where a tall potted tree stands.

To add elegance to the once unadorned mantel, Jen selected an inexpensive carving to dress up the mirror and a pair of cloisonné-look vases filled with dried flowers right.

A mix of inexpensive import-store finds adds character to the low-lying Asian-style coffee table right.

Berman chose a $3,000 hand-carved piece with inlaid glass and Chinese chow feet. At $250 Jen's alternative was certainly more affordable. Although the coffee table in the makeover room is not as dark or detailed as the inspiration room piece, it still has understated Asian lines, marked by low curved legs. In either case the lesson is the same, regardless of the style of room you are creating: "You can balance expensive antiques," Sharon says, "with pieces that are more reasonable."

A two-chair seating area across from the sofa introduces another opportunity for comfort, mixing natural textures and earth tones. A blend of traditional and exotic styles, exposed wood arms, and ribbed chenille upholstery achieves a sophisticated safari club feel.

Navigate the Space With the anchor pieces—the large rug, grand window treatments, and seating pieces—in place, it is time to draw attention to the details that give this budget-savvy exotic space character. Stacked antique suitcases from a flea market (one is an old faux-grained English tin trunk) find new function as a conversation table between the chairs. Taking the place of a traditional side table, these pieces add to the well-traveled feel of the space. In another corner of the room—and of the world—an heirloom chest huddles under a pair of prints in ornately carved wood frames, which balance the tall tree on the other side of the fireplace.

Then there's the mantel. The inspiration room's mantel was adorned with an inlaid bone and mother-of-pearl mirror—expensive touches that exude exotic elegance. Such opulence was foreign to the modest budget in the makeover space. By embellishing the built-in mirror with an inexpensive store-bought Indonesian carving and introducing two imitation cloisonné vases that frame the global picture on either side of the reflection, the less expensive version has just as much class—for a lot less cash.

Pattern Perfect

Do you love pattern but are unsure of how to mix patterns successfully? Follow these tips, and soon you'll be mixing and matching like a pro:

- **Keep in mind three is the key.** Introducing a maximum of three patterns in a space will prevent the eye from being overwhelmed.

- **Work within a limited color palette.** Sticking to just a few colors for all the patterned elements in a space will keep the look consistent and help the patterns complement—rather than compete with—one another.

- **Vary the size and scale of the patterns**—but consider them relative to the size of the room. For example, a small detailed pattern on a wallcovering in a large room would be too busy, but in a small space it is just right.

- **Remember that distribution matters.** Thoughtfully placing items of various patterns throughout a space will keep it balanced; avoid grouping patterned elements together because it will create too many focal points in a room.

- **Consider manufacturer suggestions.** Many fabric and wallcovering manufacturers offer groupings of colors and patterns that work well together. These collections are created to take the guesswork out of mixing and matching.

The centerpiece above includes separately potted orchids, dried mushrooms, moss, and palmlike plants reminiscent of flora one might find in an exotic rain forest.

The coffee table centerpiece in the thrifty makeover also offers a worldly escape with a natural arrangement of orchids, dried mushrooms, and low-lying plants that recall a lush exotic jungle. Other artifacts, such as a stone Buddha head, a stack of travel books, and an oblong silver box, represent intriguing parts of the globe.

Showcase Meaningful Souvenirs The inspiration room's sand-cast safari chandelier, Ming-style camel, and ceramic turtle all play into the travel dialogue that carries the eye around the room. While nothing could

replicate such one-of-a-kind treasures, Jen says the look is easy to accomplish.

She touched up a rusty antique light fixture, painting the leaves green, adding brown to the stems, and completing the safari look with ecru paper shades. She also shopped at local import stores to find a couch-height sea-grass elephant, an Asian frog statue, and the Buddha head; but she suggests blending in your own souvenirs to give the room personal stories to tell.

"Don't be afraid to experiment," Jen says. "If you have something shiny, add another piece that's dull or rusty. Put new with old, mix patterns and textures." The beauty of such an eclectic style is that the design is always evolving. Depending on where you go and what you bring back—even if it is simply a trip to your local import store or a flea market—your room is a living travel journal unified in color, yet as diverse as your experience.

▶ For a video demonstration of the chandelier transformation *below*, visit HGTV.com/sensiblechic

Lighting adapts easily and affordably to any motif, Jen says. Green, camel, and pearl paint accents turned a rusty old chandelier above into a tropical-style focal point.

The Look for Less

If you are ready to embark on a decorating adventure—but your budget is limited—fear not! Use these tips to help you create a room that only looks expensive.

▶ **Collect one nice piece from everywhere you go** to add meaning to your decor. Decorating with things that have meaning or stories behind them, says Jen Jordan, brings individuality to any space. Look with different eyes at heirlooms you've inherited—old books, dishware, stitchery, clothing, even your grandfather's pipe—to see how they might be displayed.

▶ **Details define the look of your room,** but such nuances need not be a part of every piece. A great compromise is to purchase more expensive or larger items in a simpler style, and then invest in design-specific accent pieces to upgrade the look.

▶ **Good rugs are costly.** Search garage sales and Internet auctions for better buys. Even with fading and wear and tear, used rugs can be cleaned and blemishes camouflaged, depending on how you place the furniture.

▶ **Add details to an inexpensive light fixture** to give it a designer look. Coat it in a bold paint color, add fringe and beads, or change the crystals. Introduce pattern and texture by stenciling and/or upholstering the existing shades, or purchase new shades for a low-cost update.

▶ **If you can't travel to foreign destinations yourself, visit ethnic shops and villages** that sell affordable handmade crafts and other decorative imports, including masks, dolls, statues, and unusual artwork.

makeover room $2,082

Lesson Five | Cater to Contrast

In any room matchy-matchy—in terms of color, texture, and shape—can be tacky-tacky. To create a room that excites the eyes and other senses, think contrast. This lesson is black and white: If carefully planned, contrast can be compelling. Select a minimal color scheme; opt for clean, simple lines; and revel in a room that speaks of style. While both bedrooms have some decidedly formal elements, it's the play on contrasts and the soothing color scheme that make each an inviting getaway. If you want to liven up a dull room in your home on a budget, employ the strategies used these rooms.

	Sensible Makeover	Inspiration
Wall Paint	$180	$50
Window Treatments	$195	$6,900
Bed	$700	$4,800
Bedding	$175	$1,482
Pillows/Shams	$80	$1,063
Dresser/Accessories	$227	$2,408
Mirrors	$70	$2,855
Bedside Lamps	$100	$2,076
Bedside Table/ Accessories/ Artwork	$68	$865
Wing Chair/Pillows	$220	$2,140
Reading Table	$67	$1,788
Bamboo Bench	*	$1,035
TOTAL	$2,082	$27,462

*The makeover room was too small to include a bench.

Build on Basic Colors When establishing contrast, it's important to introduce a limited color palette. Both the high-end room and the makeover space incorporate a basic range from white (no color at all) to taupe (the midpoint) to black (saturated color). The only exception? The walls. While all the elements of the rooms revolve around contrasting black and white, the walls require some color; without it they would be too stark and wouldn't convey a relaxed atmosphere. "When a room doesn't have a color at all, you don't feel any particular way," Jen Jordan of *Sensible Chic* explains. In the makeover room aqua blue paint is evocative: "The idea is to feel calm, fresh, and clean," she says.

inspiration room $27,462

Taking a cue from the expensive custom-designed room left, the Sensible Makeover opposite features an upholstered headboard made from the same taupe fabric as the duvet cover, which softens the bed's strong telescoping lines. Contrasting dark- and light-color furnishings balance the weight on either side in both rooms—but this lesson in contrasts was achieved for about $25,000 less than the original.

Pillows in khaki and cream fabrics add comfort to the bed above. With their shaped and embellished edges they are the only romantic features in the room—yet they blend with the color scheme so they don't detract from the overall streamlined look of the room.

Though the makeover room below right is balanced—matching lamps stand on the two bedside tables and the tall print on the right side of the room is at the same height of the mirror on the left—it has many contrasting elements in color, shape, and texture. These elements relax the formality in both the makeover room and the high-end inspiration room left.

Inspiration room designer Annie Bowman takes the idea of a limited palette further: "Even though colors are contrasting, they should harmonize." For instance, the dramatic black bedposts—sharp and contemporary in design—in both the inspiration room and the less expensive Sensible Makeover are offset by soft linen textures and neutral tones of the duvet covers. The inspiration room cover had a classic pinstripe design, but a wider stripe—that was considerably less expensive—dresses the budget-savvy bed. Although wider stripes often convey a more whimsical feel, they don't detract from the bed because of the linenlike fabric and soft color scheme. "The point was that it be a natural-looking fabric, to keep it clean and simple," Jen explains.

Jen's choice of fabrics is also utilitarian. "If you really hunt for linen, you can find it inexpensively"; however, she says, "the real savings in this choice is that it's washable." Active families with children and pets should purchase covers they can clean frequently and easily—a great tip when selecting fabrics to be used throughout the house, including slipcovers and window treatments.

Continuing the look, the same linen fabric used for the duvet also embellishes the headboard. To replicate the inspiration room design, Jen was lucky to find a headboard with a natural arch inset. "The simple contrast makes it crisp and contemporary," Jen explains. "It's not muddled in romance or pattern or anything too crazy." Piles of pillows that

Color Play

In the makeover bedroom soft aqua-color walls set the stage for relaxation. Because the furnishings and accessories could adapt readily to nearly any design style, other wall colors could achieve different impressions. For instance, red walls against the dark lines of the furnishings might suggest an Asian influence, while smoky gray or taupe would inject an urban feel. The ability to change the feel of the room simply by changing the wall color makes this design beautifully—and affordably—versatile.

The bed is the natural focal point in a bedroom, but without a headboard a bed might not command the attention it deserves. This simple yet striking project allows you to dress up your bed with a fabric that complements the other colors and patterns in your bedroom. The key is to find a headboard that has a recessed area in which you can insert an upholstered piece of plywood.

ONE: Trace the recessed design on a kraft paper template, piecing paper together if needed to create the pattern. Cut away approximately ½ inch of the pattern all around to allow for the batting and fabric (so that the upholstered portion will fit snugly in the recessed area).

TWO: Tape the paper pattern on a piece of ¼-inch plywood. Cut out. Sand the edges and wipe away any dust with a tack cloth.

THREE: Wrap polyester batting around the plywood piece; staple to the back and cut excess batting. Cover the batting-covered plywood with fabric; staple to the back and cut excess fabric.

FOUR: Place the upholstered plywood on the headboard, into the recessed area. Screw the plywood into place (through the back of the headboard).

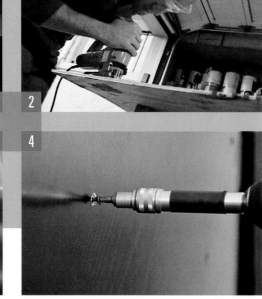

► For a video demonstration of the headboard project, visit HGTV.com/sensiblechic

rest against the headboard invite slumber. These khaki and cream-color pillows blend with the established color scheme, yet dressy details, delicate floral patterns, and tone-on-tone prints add a little romance to keep the room from feeling too formal.

Use Supporting Sidekicks When working with contrast keep balance in mind as well. "You don't want all your dark colors on one side of the room," Jen warns. "Make sure the blacks and whites are distributed equally." This will keep the visual flow of the room from hitting a "brick wall." In both rooms the side tables ground the bed in a dark wood dresser on the left and a round table with a taupe-color linen covering on the right. But, light-color accessories keep the dresser from being overbearing, and dark-color elements don't allow the round table to float away.

The inspiration room's expensive alder wood French dresser touted a detailed ebony finish, bowed details, and delicate hardware—but Jen did not expect to find such a one-of-a-kind piece with her limited budget. Instead she created her own espresso-color finish by spray-painting a neoclassic-style dresser that happened to have the right hardware in place. Toned-down dresser-top accessories—including a wood box-turned-planter with one simple white orchid, seeded ball, and vase, none of which are shiny or flashy—continue the room's organic feel. But even with these quiet features, the deep dark color of the hefty mirror frame and the dresser offer strong contrast. Reflections of the lush window treatments in the mirror also dramatize the corner.

On the right side of the bed, the

A neoclassic-style dresser left makes a strong design statement with its new dark finish. While the mirror has a complementary hefty frame, the other accessories, such as the cream-color lamp and potted orchid, have a lighter, more organic feel.

At just $68 with accessories, the round side table below with a taupe linen cloth is the room's best buy—compared to $865 for the inspiration-room table. The deep wood tones of the box and the shapely vase contrast in both color and texture.

Decorating Do-Overs

When decorating a room, use furniture and accent designs that can be changed or adapted so that getting a whole new look is as easy as swapping out fabric. For example, if the homeowners want to take this bedroom from relaxing to invigorating, they can easily reupholster the headboard with fabric of another color, pattern, or texture (for instance, a fabric with bold warm-tone flowers or stripes). The same is true of drop-in dining chair seats (which typically require only a small amount of fabric), slipcovers for any furnishing, and even pillows. If the basic shape and lines of the furnishings or decorative elements are clean and simple, they can adapt to any decorating style.

Mirror, Mirror

The reflective quality of mirrors puts them in a decorating class all their own. When shopping for a mirror consider the following:

- **Practical or pretty?** Mirrors are functional when used for personal hygiene: applying makeup or jewelry, shaving, or styling hair. They also can be used to open up a room that has little natural light, make cramped corners feel larger, or help tables appear more elegant. In this room propping a mirror over the side dresser doubles the light in the corner. The white orchid and lamp reflected in the mirror draw attention to the contrasts.

- **Sizing up.** The size of the piece over which your mirror hangs or stands should dictate the height and width of the mirror. As a rule, the mirror should always be narrower than or equal to—never wider than—the width of the furniture. Hang or prop the mirror at eye level, unless you are grouping it with other items for specific design purposes.

- **Reflections on style.** Choose a mirror that works with the rest of the room. In this case the bed is substantial in its weight and dark color, so the mirror is of comparable substance. With a scrollwork bed, a mirror with a delicate frame might be more fitting.

- **Playing with the plane.** Experiment with mirrors on different surfaces and different planes. For instance, arrange candles, vases, or perfume bottles on a mirror that lies flat on a dresser. Hang a mirror in an unsuspecting corner, such as on the wall of a stair landing or dormer, to add interest to overlooked spaces.

opposite holds true; there are no defined lines as with the dresser and mirror. The soft, round shape of the taupe-covered table differentiates itself from the bold bed and dresser, while the cost is equally attractive. Covering a table with a remnant of fabric "is a great economical solution and a chance to use another textile," Jen says. Streamlined white lamps and a few accessories add tabletop detail without complicating the look.

The window treatments are a perfect combination of drama (black velvet curtains that echo the black bed and dresser) and quiet (cream-color sheers). These treatments differ in weight, color, and texture, yet in combination they offer the homeowners both natural light and sunshine for daytime activities and total darkness at night.

Use Space Productively Bedrooms are often used for more than just sleeping, and carving out a corner for any activity—such as reading, exercising, or home computing—doesn't need to take up a lot of space or cost a lot of money. In this bedroom a small space to the right of the bed is the perfect place for a cozy reading corner. In the spirit of the inspiration room's down-cushioned wing chair, the makeover room offers an equally comfortable, low-maintenance seat—priced at almost $2,000 less. Its eggshell-color slipcover can be easily removed for washing, while the handmade pillows sewn from embroidered tea towels add inviting details. A scrolled metal table with a black metal top repeats the curves of the nearby round table, and a silver vase filled with large white roses completes the corner.

The Look for Less

Getting a high-end look for less in your bedroom—or any room in your home—is easy when you learn these basic design and decorating principles:

- ▶ **Use memories of vacations or cues from a movie in a faraway land to set the stage** for your decorating dream—but you don't have to take the style too literally. When inspiration room designer Annie Bowman envisioned this room, she had just returned from a trip to France. Influenced by Paris flea market trends and textures, she says, "So many pieces were covered in linen; they were so simple and had so much style." Because linen is costly, a mix of linen-look and cotton fabrics is featured in the Sensible Makeover space—but the resulting look is no less stunning.

- ▶ **When shopping for bed linens, keep your lifestyle in mind.** Dry-clean-only fabrics may be impractical in a home with active kids, frequent guests, and roaming pets. Instead, look for multiweave, washable fabrics that require less care. For the makeover room *Sensible Chic*'s Jen Jordan chose a linen blend for the duvet cover that still has a natural color and texture but is easier to maintain than the real thing.

- ▶ **To add bulk to a bed**—for a more luxurious, hotel-like look—without much expense, purchase one comforter for sleeping and a separate decorative cover for the foot of the bed. Fold the decorative cover in half or thirds to add height, color, and texture.

- ▶ **Approach any container as a possible planter.** "You can put flowers in anything to create interesting design points," Jen suggests. An orchid in a wooden box adds height and natural interest on the bedside dresser in this bedroom.

- ▶ **Inexpensive round decorator tables can soften the look of any room** and provide an opportunity to introduce texture with a covering. Here, the round shape and taupe linen tablecloth balance the strong lines of the bedposts and dark-painted dresser on the opposite side of the bed.

- ▶ **Be creative when accessorizing with pillows.** The plush cushions tossed on the reading chair are fashioned from embroidered tea towels that were cut and sewn to fit a manufactured pillow form. Recycle old clothing (such as jeans with pockets for a child's room or an apron for a kitchen chair), or stitch together kitchen towels, napkins, or canvas carryalls for budget-savvy accents in any room in your home.

The easy chair's eggshell-color canvas slipcover is washable and resistant to fading in sunlight. Plush pillows and a black metal table work together to create contrast in this cozy corner.

makeover room $2,516

Harmony + Unity = Sophisticated Style

Similar shapes and compatible colors that are in tune with each other create a relaxing visual rhythm—and both the high-price inspiration room and Sensible Makeover featured here sing with style. The design for the expensive original began with a window view overlooking calming natural gardens. "We wanted to bring that feeling into the room," says inspiration room designer Alison Whittaker. Color, texture, and clean lines flow from one piece to another in both spaces, with all the elements uniting for a calming bedroom retreat —yet the looks of these two rooms were created at very different prices. If you desire a serene space that's pulled together—and affordable—follow the design cues on the following pages.

	Sensible Makeover	Inspiration
Wall Paint	$50	$45
Window Treatments/Hardware	$170	$775
Bed	$650	$3,000
Duvet Cover/Bedding	$330	$2,050
Pillows	$42	$725
Side Table/Accessories	$240	$3,301
Artwork	$100	$2,500
Bedside Lamps	$140	$3,000
Dresser/Accessories	$267	$3,815
Bench	$115	$775
Console Table/Accessories	$352	$10,669
Candelier	$60	$2,750
TOTAL	$2,516	$33,405

Think Organic: Color and Texture Although the design of both the high-price inspiration room and the less costly makeover room is distinctly sophisticated, the combination of elements exudes a sense of nature. The inspiration room walls were bathed in an earthy greenish brown, but *Sensible Chic's* Jen Jordan painted the makeover room taupe. "It's understated, yet provides a feeling of intimacy and being embraced. It's a very flexible, intelligent color," Jen says. Both hues offer a quiet background on which to build a relaxed retreat. All the colors in the Sensible Makeover room instill harmony. "They're all medium values, and the textures are complementary," Jen explains.

The sleigh bed in the inspiration room

Both the high-cost inspiration room right and the budget-savvy makeover space left are filled with streamlined shapes. Taupe and gold tones repeated on the walls and bedding— along with natural, organic elements—create a relaxed visual rhythm.

inspiration room $33,405

Chenille and embossed-fabric pillows above add texture to the bed. The small pillow in front repeats the darker values in the headboard and offers pleasing contrast against the shimmery dupioni silk duvet cover.

cover. And the darker patchwork pillow, positioned front and center, offers a burst of warm red against the neutral-color bedding—upping the tempo just a bit. This subtle mixture of color, pattern, and texture is subdued enough to soothe the soul, yet exciting enough to keep the room from appearing boring.

To complement the earthy look—and introduce an organic material—a natural-fiber Roman shade in the inspiration room filtered the light. Jen chose a less expensive variation, using natural matchstick blinds for one window and khaki-color panels that blend with the wall color to frame the focal-point bed.

featured caning and rattan, along with a mix of sultry curves and bold contemporary lines, that convey a modern Asian feel. This bed was a commanding focal point in the room. "Its curves have an appeal that runs from traditional to contemporary designs," Alison says. Although the makeover room bed is not custom-crafted, its tailored shape and dark espresso wood still establish a strong modern presence. And, like the expensive original, the budget-friendly bed has a tall dark wood frame that lifts the bed and increases its visibility.

Textured bedding and a mix of pillows soften the look in each room. In the inspiration room luxurious dupioni silk, velvet, and patterned applique work in harmony, and complementary colors unify the grouping. "It's good to mix and match," Jen says. Sage-color chenille Euro pillows in the makeover space are soft and inviting. Two leaf-pattern pillows continue the nature theme while repeating the lustrous texture of the dupioni silk duvet

Create Movement When designing any room, use the lines and colors of the furnishings and accessories to carry the eye on a visual tour. Help the eye move from one piece to another at a pace that suits the mood you want to create in the space—from a calm Sunday afternoon drive to a high-energy thrill ride.

At the head of each bed, the bold colors and sharp lines of the graphic prints draw the eye to a higher level—further promoting the bed as the main feature of the room. Concurrently the earth tones keep the pace relaxed. Because the budget could not support a valuable painting, Jen took the brush into her own hands. With an inexpensive rendition of the original as a springboard and using the lines as a guide, she painted over the existing design in coordinating acrylic paints. In both rooms the artwork adds graphic appeal in warm tones that contrast with the neutral-color surroundings.

In both the inspiration room and the

Backed by natural matchstick blinds, the altar table accessories left find harmony with nature. Each piece has simple, strong lines, yet together they are light and airy in front of the window.

Side table accessories all encourage harmony with the world. Iron birds are symbols of life and peace, three bamboo stalks are considered good luck, and a white orb suggests purity and simplicity.

Personalized Furnishings

Inexpensive furniture often looks the part with mass-produced motifs and contrived details. *Sensible Chic's* Jen Jordan advises that you alter a piece whenever you can, but be careful not to cover attractive wood grain. "It's always worth it to customize it yourself," she explains. "Then the piece becomes one of a kind."

- **Paint.** Look for patterns and natural lines in a piece that can serve as guidelines for painting different colors or designs. You may paint some portions of a piece and leave other portions in a natural finish.

- **Stencil or stamp.** Explore crafts stores for stencil and stamp motifs that complement any decor style.

- **Embellish.** Apply unusual hardware, such as knobs, handles, and decorative trims, to add personality to any piece. Gold leafing, tile, and decoupage papers offer other finishing options. But be sure to think about how the piece will be used, considering durability, washability, and compatibility with room design before investing time and money in any embellishment project.

Sensible Makeover space, the bench at the foot of the bed helps create rhythm by moving the eye down from the bed toward another texture. Jen found the makeover bench with a rattan-style base at a discount store. "It looks Asian inspired," she explains. To help the piece mimic the colors and textures already established in the space, she makes a few

quick, easy alterations: Jen painted the base in an espresso color that repeats the wood tones throughout the room and re-covered the existing cushion with a patterned fabric that complements the pillows.

To anchor the arrangement and offer practical storage space, side tables continue the movement on either side of the bed. "Only when a room is extremely modern," Jen says, "do the pieces have to match. In fact, it's more appropriate that they don't match." In both the high-price room and the budget-savvy makeover, one table has open shelves and the other has drawers, yet their simple lines and consistent color make them work together.

To bring the eye full circle, a candelier above the bed reinforces the quiet mood of the room and joins the bedside lamps in the lighting pool. The version in the inspiration room was electrified; however, the less expensive fixture that the *Sensible Chic* crew fabricated is just as visually compelling. A 24-inch-diameter base, painted in a bronze hue, serves as the foundation for a ring of pillar candles that are set on glass candle trays. The candelier hangs on chains from the center of the ceiling. (See page 28 for instructions.)

Unify the Theme The tranquil outdoor garden influence enhances the Asian look and is a fitting direction for the soothing spaces. An altar table under the window becomes a secondary destination point; it is appealing for its organic materials and modest tabletop landscape. The inspiration piece, a centuries-old Ming Dynasty-style work, had a rosewood base and a 3-inch-thick hand-lacquered top. It is an impressive piece—but with a price of almost $10,000 it was far from the reach of the *Sensible Chic* team. To mimic the look of the original, Jen purchased an inexpensive console table at a Chinese import store. She painted the top portion a cream

SENSIBLE PROJECT
Presto Change-o Artwork

Inexpensive prints abound at crafts and chain department stores, making it easy to change artwork on a whim. If you've already made an investment in a print or poster you love, but you want to change the style of the room it resides in, you're in luck: Pick up some paint and alter the look of the piece in minutes.

ONE: Remove the print from its frame; if needed, set the glass aside. Using spray paint that's formulated for the frame material (i.e., wood or metal), apply one or two thin, even coats of paint to the frame; let dry.

TWO: Choose a color palette that complements the new look you want to achieve. Pour small amounts of acrylic paints onto a paper plate. Use an artist's paintbrush to paint over the existing print, using a clean brush for each paint color; let dry.

THREE: Reframe and rehang the print.

color and the base black. The resulting look is serene and clean, especially with a pared-down collection of accessories that has a place and a purpose in the overall design.

The accessories present throughout the room are important to the look, which Alison stresses must be simple in a serene setting. "You can't clutter the space with little things that don't relate," she explains. "Set things on the table that are pleasing to the eye to create a sort of three-dimensional painting. You have to be selective." By being choosy it is easier to create a sense of harmony in a space; cluttering a display with unrelated items creates design dissonance.

Incorporating Asian-looking flora—such as lucky bamboo stalks and a bonsailike plant—brings touches of the outdoors in. A square candle on a square base repeats the simple strong lines present elsewhere in the room; the repetition of shape keeps the serene space unified. Metal birds and a bronze bowl introduce additional organic elements. The lamps on the side tables have a more contemporary feel with their brushed-silver bases and clean-lined shades; however, they provide some height and lots of visual impact—yet not so much that they are out of tune in the room. In all, the accessories are in sync with one another and work

The serene space right is a mix of many styles—contemporary-style furnishings, a symmetrical arrangement of elements that's a nod to traditional, and earthly Asian-inspired colors and accents. But by paying attention to clean lines and harmonizing colors and textures, the Sensible Chic team created a room that feels pulled together, not undone.

together to achieve harmony.

By paring down the number of accessories in the space—and choosing elements that share a common ground, such as color, shape, and line—plus toning down the strong-line, dark-color furnishings with neutral colors and soft textures, the space is a relaxing place to unwind. In a fast-paced world with unlimited design choices, the unified calm provides a welcome diversion.

▶ For a video demonstration of the candelier project *opposite*, visit HGTV.com/sensiblechic

Jen gave a custom look to this console table above by painting the top a cream color and the base black. "This is the strongest Asian piece in the room," she says. Its sloped ends are reminiscent of pagoda architecture.

The Look for Less

If you dream of a space that's dressed to the nines—but you need to decorate on a dime—follow these guidelines for high style on a budget.

▶ **When in doubt about color, choose taupe,** which *Sensible Chic*'s Jen Jordan says is a sophisticated choice. The deeper the shade, the more drama it denotes.

▶ **Accomplish a luxurious look without the luxurious price:** Blend textures and tones, spending more on the most important element, and less on the accent pieces. In the budget-friendly room, for instance, Jen invested in a gold dupioni silk bedspread but then mixed and matched less expensive pillows with interesting textures and embellishments.

▶ **The altar table in the inspiration room was made of organic materials** and served as a prominent piece of art. When you use less costly pieces, Jen says, "Try to add elements of craftsmanship. Take every opportunity to paint or add." In this case painting the base of the table black and the tabletop cream gives a thrifty console a custom look.

▶ **Shop in your house before you go shopping.** The nicest accessories are those that have personal meaning. Find new uses for old things: Remove cups or bowls from the china cabinet and display them on shelves, or fill a glass vase with colored marbles from your childhood.

▶ **Fresh bamboo stalks are wonderfully compatible with Asian designs.** Buy the tropical woody stems from a local florist and place them in water as you would cut flowers, and they'll continue to grow. They are low maintenance, introduce soft organic lines to a room, and you'll enjoy the added lore of bringing good luck.

▶ **Metal accents don't have to match;** it's fine to mix metals, Jen says, as long as they look organic and earthy and are not overly polished.

makeover room $2,482

Lesson Seven | Theme Decorating

As more people travel the world—or are exposed to global customs via television and the Internet—our decorating styles are undoubtedly influenced. Designing a room around any given place can establish a connection to one's family heritage or simply reflect a favorite culture. From African safari to Moroccan menagerie, every style communicates a mood—and any one of them is easily accessible with the shops and resources we have at our disposal. In both the high-cost inspiration room and the Sensibly Chic makeover space, cheery colors, lively patterns, and rustic-style furnishings invoke the spirit of the relaxed countryside of Southern France. If you desire a French provincial getaway—or want to capture the mood of any location throughout the world—look to these spaces for strategies to put your decorating dreams in motion.

Perk Up with Color and Fabric When we dream of faraway lands, we don't see in black and white—our eyes are opened to a world of color, texture, and pattern.

Inspiration room designer Penny Chin describes the inspiration room as stylized French Provence: With its color palette of soft yellows, reds, and blues,

	Sensible Makeover	Inspiration
Built-In Cabinets	*	$8,500
Window Treatments	$123	$2,100
Window Cabinet/Shelves	$390	*
Shelf Accessories	$91	$1,373
Wine Cabinet	$300	*
Wine Cabinet Accessories	$147	$1,646
Table	$250	$4,500
Chairs	$585	$11,880
Tabletop Accessories	$326	$3,395
Rug	$250	$12,980
Sconce Shades	$20	*
TOTAL	$2,482	$46,374

*Built-in window cabinetry and a wall hutch were preexisting in the inspiration room. To replicate the look for less in the makeover room, a large sideboard, wine cabinet, and decorative shelves are installed. The inspiration room did not have wall sconces, but the existing sconces in the makeover room are retained.

inspiration room $46,374

Characteristic of southern France's Provençe region, small floral prints, rustic wood furnishings, and a mix of sunny colors create a comfortable dining domain. This relaxed mood is captured in both the costly inspiration room left and the less expensive—but just as charming—makeover space opposite.

Setting the Scene

To capture the mood of a place or period in time, almost everything in the room should center around the colors, patterns, and styles of that period.

- **Do your homework.** Collect magazine clippings, explore books and the Internet, and visit antique stores to learn about the objects, icons, colors, and furnishings that best represent the chosen theme.

- **Pay attention when you travel.** Visit museums, talk to locals, and notice the details of different cultures whenever you travel. Keep a journal, take pictures, and purchase postcards reminding you of the looks you like. If international travel is not in your budget, explore local import stores and seek out special exhibits at museums for a glimpse into any given culture.

- **Watch movies set in the location.** To ensure a movie set looks authentic, set designers must conduct research—and you can benefit from their hard work by closely examining the elements you see on the big screen. This will give you hints as to the fabrics, colors, and furnishings you should incorporate into your design.

The valance fabric below is more English than French, Jen says, but the soft color and delicate floral print evoke feelings of the countryside. A pleat made of raspberry red linen adds contrast and interest to the simple design.

the space is a relaxed and sophisticated take on this region. According to *Sensible Chic*'s Jen Jordan, this look is "within our comfort zone, charming and traditional with a lot of color"—which makes it a favorite for homes across the nation.

Penny used color as the inspiration room's springboard, beginning with buttery yellow paint on the walls. A comparable yellow also sets a fresh, casual tone in the Sensibly Chic dining room. "It's definitely a happy yellow," Jen explains. Choosing a soft hue for the walls allows the fabrics and furnishings to be the main focus, and

the yellow ushers in feelings of warmth and sunshine better than white walls could ever do. The lesson is this: Regardless of what theme you want to re-create in your home, look to colors—on the walls, for the fabrics, and on the floor—to help tell the story, whether it's bold reds for an Asian-inspired space or lively jewel tones for a Moroccan-styled room.

In both the inspiration and makeover rooms, large windows on two walls allow natural light to enter. To maximize the brightness—and not conceal the view—Penny had valances made of an English floral fabric for the inspiration room; although the cheery fabric she chose isn't truly provincial, it still adds European flavor. Jen found a less expensive floral-print fabric for the valances in the makeover space that worked just as well. "If you're trying to get the feeling of a culture or ethnic style," she says, "you still can use things from other places. Relaxing the style makes the room look more believable." To prevent the soft yellow used on the walls and window treatments from becoming too flat and boring, bold touches of raspberry red are tucked into the box pleats. This use of color adds dimension to the treatments and offers pleasing contrast.

At the center of the inspiration room, an antique Oriental rug offsets the tile and wood floor pattern—and adds bold color and pattern—for a price of $12,980. Jen replicated the look for a mere $250 with a variation that she purchased at an estate sale. Although the less expensive version isn't as large

A wine cabinet that has been painted yellow fits the narrow space under existing wall sconces above left. A glass front adds dimension and offers a stylish way to display favorite dishware.

Jen painted a store-bought sideboard above right yellow—the same color as the walls—to make it resemble the built-in unit in the inspiration room. Topping it with topiaries and a bowl of fresh fruit establishes the provincial theme.

Jen re-covered the seats of six ladder-back chairs with cotton fabric in a yellow plaid design. Cushioned backs on the two head chairs make the grouping feel like a custom set right.

"There isn't room for a big china cabinet," Jen explains, so shelves are introduced to offer additional display space below. By hammering nails into a shelf (and allowing about an inch to be visible on the top), the dishes stand upright without the need to cut a special groove.

The top is left with its original warm wood tone, to further replicate the look of the expensive version. To duplicate the storage space of the built-in cabinet, the *Sensible Chic* team added shelves on the walls above the sideboard. These showcase dishware and other heirlooms, while the top of the sideboard is used to display tall topiaries and a bowl of fruit.

On the wall adjacent to the window, Jen placed a wine cabinet under a pair of sconces. The cabinet had a dark finish, but when painted the same sunny yellow as the sideboard, the piece looks custom-made for the space. She placed a pair of tall, heavy candlesticks on the wine cabinet to balance the topiaries that stand on the adjacent sideboard and add importance to this side of the room. Shelves over the wine cabinet provide another display area and help create a charming vignette.

Together the sideboard and wine cabinet create an intimate feeling, wrapping furniture around the room and enveloping the dining area. Although the pieces had dissimilar appearances, painting them makes them seem like companions. Because both pieces have strong lines and hefty hardware, they complement the other rustic-style furnishings in the

▶ For a video demonstration of the dining chair project, visit HGTV.com/sensiblechic

as the original, it still works: "Oriental rugs anchor a room in an old-world way," Jen says. And, as a bonus, their busy patterns help hide stains and coordinate easily with most color schemes.

Create a Custom Look Because the expertly crafted built-in cabinets in the inspiration room were too expensive for the makeover room, Jen found other affordable options that offer storage and areas for display. Positioned below a large picture window, a store-bought pine sideboard takes the place of the marble-top counter and hutch unit that graces the high-price room. Painting the less expensive piece yellow—the same color as the wall—creates the effect of a permanent fixture.

room. The bottom line: Regardless of what decorating theme you are working toward, look for furnishings that have simple lines. The addition of hardware, embellishments, or paint that is reminiscent of the theme can transport the look to anywhere across the globe.

Make a Feast for the Eyes Now that the perimeter and floor of each room have been dressed in casual French-country elegance, it's time to turn attention to the main feature of the space: the dining table and seating. The tables used in both spaces speak to an old-world style. The 19th-century version that proudly stands in the inspiration room is set on curvaceous iron legs. The oak-planked top has a rustic appearance that's perfect for a country-style space. Even without the scrollwork details, Jen's alternative manages to communicate a rustic feel with its soft wood tones and strong lines—for thousands less.

In the inspiration room six antique chairs offer diners a comfortable place to enjoy a meal. The dining chairs in the Sensibly Chic space resemble the expensive originals, thanks to light-tone wood frames, a mix of straight and curvy shapes, and similar upholstery. The chairs in both spaces are dressed in a lighthearted plaid fabric that easily adds to the pattern mix: The same soft yellow present throughout both spaces is the predominant color. Jen re-covered the drop-in dining seats in the *Sensible Chic* room and added upholstered backs to two of the chairs to further capture the look of the costly originals.

In both spaces, color and accessories

Creating a custom look for your dining room doesn't have to cost a fortune: Follow the steps below to re-cover a drop-in seat with ease and make a padded backing for any wood chair. Select a fabric for this project that has a tight weave that can stand up to stretching and, if the chair will be used frequently, make sure the fabric you choose can be cleaned easily.

ONE: To re-cover a drop-in seat, remove the seat from the chair. Remove the staples that hold the existing fabric in place. Place the new fabric right side down; place the old fabric on the new fabric, pin in place, and cut out. **Note:** If the old batting is worn-out, purchase new batting and cut to the size of the new fabric. Center the seat on the batting (if added) and fabric, right side down. Starting at one side, pull the fabric to the underside of the seat and staple the center of the fabric edge. Repeat on all remaining sides, pulling the fabric taut. Continue stapling around the fabric until it is secured; at the corners, neatly fold and staple. Trim any excess fabric and replace the seat in the chair.

TWO: To make a back for a chair, trace the outline of the chair back (within the frame) onto kraft paper; cut out. Trace the template onto $1/4$-inch plywood; cut out with a jigsaw. Place the plywood on the chair to check the fit. Cover the plywood front and back, following the directions for the drop-in seat above. Screw the plywood into the front of the chair frame. Using fabric glue, adhere fabric trim to the upholstered plywood, concealing the screws.

With its traditional floral print, the table runner right is a key French element. Etched hurricane lamps, a chicken canister, a pot of lavender, and ceramic and pewter dishes support the casual country style—and closely mimic the more costly antiques used to dress the table in the inspiration room below.

are key to creating a French country scene, but such decorative elements can be altered to help you successfully re-create any look from across the globe right in your home. "Make the eye feel like it's being bathed with exciting color," Penny says. Given the resulting casual tone, you don't need to travel far to appreciate the pleasant French Provençe influence of these two dining rooms. Perhaps most important in communicating a sense of Provençe is the use of traditional French accessories, table linens, and dishware.

In the inspiration room a mix of yellow, white, and blue dishware mingles with pewter and tall, elegant glass candlesticks. The look is sophisticated but casual. While it would be easy to allow the table settings to consume a large part of a dining room budget, Jen proves that less expensive French reproductions are just as convincing as the originals. Mimicking the inspiration room, the table runner in the Sensibly Chic space is a focal point, decorating the tabletop with a traditional French print. A basket of lavender continues the country theme, while inexpensive pottery and pewter accents—including a chicken canister—recall local cottage industry influence.

"The table is purposely set informally," Jen says. Mismatched blue and white pieces introduce calming contrast to the surrounding yellows and reds. Wine glasses and napkins add touches of blue, while the hurricane glasses that surround large pillar candles have an etched surface that repeats the delicate patterns on the dishware and table runner. Together, all these elements combine to say French country casual with just the right accent.

The Look for Less

Regardless of the style of room you desire, there are tips and tricks the professionals use to get a high-end look for less. Here's a sampling of the very best ideas you can use today.

▶ **When your space and/or budget do not lend themselves to custom built-in cabinetry, imitate the look with store-bought furniture painted to match the walls.** For the Sensibly Chic room, Jen Jordan purchased an inexpensive sideboard and wine cabinet and painted them the same buttery yellow as the walls. This technique makes the pieces appear as though they had always been a part of the space.

▶ **To add display space to a room—without spending a lot for cabinetry—add shapely shelves, as the *Sensible Chic* team did.** Use the shelves to showcase treasures or display items you use daily, positioning them so you can easily access them when needed.

▶ **Although Jen bought the country table new, if you're handy, you can also cut corners by piecing together a separate tabletop and base.** Salvage mismatched pieces such as wrought-iron scrollwork legs at flea markets and garage sales. If you can't find a top, design your own surface from reclaimed lumber. Rather than buying new, look for an old table with a wood finish that looks worn and comfortable, not shiny and bright.

▶ **With its colors, motifs, and textures, fabric can have powerful impact—and evoke various moods and attitudes—in any space.** To add a splash of cultural elegance to your dining room, purchase an embroidered silk for an Asian-style space or sturdy mudcloth for an African theme and re-cover the drop-in chair seats, following the steps on page 67.

▶ **For a rustic European look, comb garage sales, estate sales, flea markets, and antiques stores to accessorize inexpensively.** For other looks—such as Japanese and Moroccan, whose beautiful objects tend to be valued treasures—seek out reproductions at local import stores.

makeover room $2,740

Lesson Eight Sizing Up the Furniture

Every room requires functional furnishings: A bedroom needs a bed, while a dining room requires a table and seating. But when it comes to selecting the right furnishings for any given room—and then arranging them in the most useful way—things can get tricky if the space is small. Inspiration room designer Jeanese Rowell created drama in a small dining area: Rich colors, bold accent pieces, and a well-planned layout maximize every inch of the room. Although the original space cost more than $82,000, *Sensible Chic* designer Jen Jordan replicated the elegance for tens of thousands less in a space that formerly served as a playroom. With an eye on price and an instinct for style, she assembled a similar room that teaches grand design lessons you can use to transform a room in your home with ease.

Create Intimacy Jeanese has decorated her share of dining rooms, but this one was particularly challenging. "It really had no empty walls," she explains. With a large built-in buffet cabinet, two walls of windows, and an open doorway, available wall space was scarce. "There's so little place for pattern or movement," Jeanese adds, surprised by the room's limiting dimensions given its location in a generous

	Sensible Makeover	Inspiration
Paint/Wall Treatment	$150	$1,350
Window Treatments/ Hardware	$410	$5,200
Rug	*	$16,500
China Cabinet/ Sideboard/Porcelain	$453	$975
Columns/Urns	$230	$540
Chandelier	$200	$15,000
Dining Table	$500	$22,500
Chairs	$505	$17,400
Tabletop Accessories	$48	$1,181
Dishes/Stemware/ Napkins	$244	$1,382
TOTAL	$2,740	$82,028

*The rug was preexisting in the makeover room.

Opulence and sophistication—velvet drapes with gold detailing, English needlepoint chair covers, and an antique rug from Pakistan—characterize the inspiration room right, which cost more than $82,000 to create. For just a fraction of the cost, the Sensible Makeover room left still has all the panache of the original, but incorporates much less costly furnishings and decorative elements.

inspiration room $82,028

Furniture Basics

How do you create a space that's stylish and comfortable? Both inspiration room designer Jeanese Rowell and *Sensible Chic*'s Jen Jordan agree: To create a space that's both beautiful and functional, evaluate how you want to use the room (for entertaining, relaxing, etc.) and what furnishings you require to make it compatible with your lifestyle:

- **Balance the center by adding elements around the perimeter.** In the case of both the inspiration room and the Sensibly Chic dining space, a large china cabinet tips the room off balance because there are no other furnishings. Adding urns with tall floral arrangements on either side of the window in the makeover room redistributes the weight and provides bursts of color and some height to the space—concurrently the slender shape of the urns allows good traffic flow.

- **Think more is better.** "The bigger your elements, the more impact you create within the room," Jeanese says. "Rooms should be convenient and embracing, so let a room serve its purpose to the maximum." By incorporating one large furnishing in a small space—such as the tall sideboard and cabinet unit in the Sensibly Chic room—you can create a sense of grandeur. Just be sure to balance a large piece with elements of comparable size and scale (for instance, using window treatments hung high on a wall).

- **Vary the height of the elements in the room** to move the eye up and down throughout the space.

- **Maximize your entertaining capacity by offering as many seats as are comfortably possible.** In a dining room smaller chairs can allow additional diners to join the table. Look for ways of increasing capacity through sectionals, leaves, and modules.

English manor. Naturally, the size of the room and the architectural elements dictated that the space be cozy, but the trick was not to make it feel cramped.

Because a dining room is meant for socializing, Jeanese says she wanted the room to be enveloping. "I tend to be large but understated," she explains, using color and furnishings to make a statement. First, she chose a round antique reproduction table that could accommodate eight to ten chairs. A rectangular shape would have divided the room in half, whereas the round table takes up less space and allows ample room all around for diners to walk and easily converse with one another. Using a round table is a great design strategy whenever there is limited space.

Jen found a similar sturdy round table with a piecrust edge, rope detailing on the legs, and a dark finish. While her version was much less expensive, the details give the piece a luxurious look. By positioning the table directly in the middle of the room, it is evenly lit by the chandelier above and is within easy reach of the sideboard. There is also ample room for smooth traffic flow around the space.

Antique needlepoint cushions of various floral motifs continue the opulent, formal look on the reproduction English Chippendale chairs in the inspiration room. To create the same handwoven look in the makeover room, Jen re-covered the drop-in seats of inexpensive chairs with remnants of brocade and jacquard. The pieces, in 1- to 2-yard lengths, are ideal for reupholstering projects and can save a great deal on a limited budget, Jen says. (See page 67 for instructions on re-covering a drop-in dining chair seat.)

A round dining table anchors the space and serves as the "social center" of the room *left*. The feature furnishing is joined by elegant dining chairs that are covered with a variety of floral fabric remnants. The fabrics resemble the vintage tapestries covering the seats of the inspiration room chairs *below*. The entire ensemble is surrounded by warm color on the walls and in the window treatments.

Close the Circle When arranging furnishings in a room, balance from the center out. The table in both spaces acts as the core, and the elements on the perimeter envelop and support it. The elaborate built-in buffet in the inspiration room wasn't possible for the *Sensible Chic* team's limited budget, but Jen made do with a splendid substitute. "We felt like we needed one substantial piece for display," Jen says. She married a mismatched sideboard and cabinet that together visually balance the tall windows on the opposite and adjacent walls—for less than $500. Although the pieces weren't intended to go together, their similar

A mismatched cabinet and sideboard left are a much more affordable alternative to the inspiration room's original built-in wall unit. The blue and white pieces—which fit comfortably in any traditional setting—are given a prominent place in the cabinet.

Fabulous Finishes

Putting a custom high-end look on inexpensive decorative accessories is quick and easy with materials from your local crafts or hardware store. To get the rich look of the columns in the inspiration room, the *Sensible Chic* team simply spray-painted plaster columns with gold, bronze, and black, in varying amounts, to create an antiqued, tarnished appearance *below left*. Look for a wide range of spray paints in a rainbow of colors and formulated to work on many surfaces—from metal to plastic—to complement your decorating scheme.

Painting an ordinary column left with a mix of rich-looking colors gives it flair for little expense.

wood tones and lines make a perfect pair. As an added bonus, the cabinet is already wired for lighting, allowing Asian-inspired blue and white pieces to have a prominent place in the room.

Pedestals with urns and tall floral arrangements create movement from the windows. "They're the best way to pull you back to the wall, so you're not overpowered by the built-in [in the inspiration room]," Jeanese explains. The urns in the makeover space are key to making the room look full and balanced: Willow twigs, berry branches, and gladiolas add smatterings of color to the light-tone walls and introduce some organic shapes to contrast with the strong lines of the furnishings.

Style on the Surface While the table and chairs set the tone for a formal dining experience, the golden wall color adds warmth and draws the eye to the room's perimeter. Yet Jeanese wasn't satisfied with warmth alone in the inspiration room; she wanted movement. "I tried to get away from plainness," she says. Even though the inspiration room was small, Jeanese selected a large acanthus pattern to paint on the wall: The monochromatic scheme keeps it from being too distracting, and the scale and size help create movement and a touch of romance. Jen used three different colors of paint—clay, dusty brown, and soft yellow highlights—to re-create the flowing motifs in the Sensibly Chic

space. While hand painting offers a free-flowing design on the walls, this look can easily be accomplished with stencils available at crafts and art supply stores.

With the walls dressed in warm color and swirling pattern, the floor also required an eye-catching treatment. Hints of the same colors used throughout both spaces are continued in the rugs, which add warmth to the wood floors and establish the table as the main feature of each space. An antique rug from Pakistan graced the inspiration room floor—at a price of $16,500. This was one way the *Sensible Chic* team could save money: The homeowners already owned an Oriental-style rug. Although it is not as large or elaborate as the expensive original, its Oriental feel still makes it a great companion for the space.

The inspiration room windows are framed in luxurious velvet drapes with gold embroidered detailing and white sheers. Together the two treatments allow light

"Don't be afraid of a bold pattern or color," Jeanese says. Jen's comparable yet less expensive gold chargers and traditional floral plates add sophistication to the table right.

Jen painted the store-bought chandelier below a golden hue and removed the amber crystals. Clear crystals alone are more formal, she explains, and allow the eye to see through to the walls.

to enter the space, yet don't disturb the view. "The draperies pull your eye out from the center and add dimension from top to bottom," Jeanese explains. Taking the lead from the inspiration room, the windows in the makeover space are flanked with rich cranberry-color velvet drapes and soft taupe sheers to establish privacy.

Accessorize with Asian Flair While English-style furnishings ground each room and help create visual flow, Asian-influence accessories give both rooms personality. Of the formal inspiration dining room, Jeanese says, "I didn't want to overdo it with a lot of things. We had tall, strong

pieces." Classic blue and white Asian ware on the table and in the china cabinet communicate traditional style without adding too much color or an overwhelming pattern to the mix. Jen was able to find less expensive blue and white reproduction pieces that stand in the cabinet and act as a centerpiece on the table. With no other china competing for attention in the room, the arrangements resemble museum-quality displays.

The chandeliers in each room serve as grand focal points. With its large scale

▶ For a video demonstration of how to re-cover chair seats, visit HGTV.com/sensiblechic

and reflective crystals, the original Italian fixture is alluring and exudes an opulent feel—at a price of $15,000. To find such a beautifully crafted piece for the makeover room was challenging, but the *Sensible Chic* team fixed up a radiant substitute: Jen removed strands of amber crystals from a comparable chandelier with metal leaf details, leaving only the largest clear crystal drops. She also painted the $200 find in a golden hue to more closely resemble the original. While the Sensibly Chic version isn't as large as the expensive one, it suits the size and scale of the room and the furnishings perfectly.

Finally, the table settings in each space celebrate all the colors in the rooms with vibrant floral patterns in red, yellow, and green. In the inspiration room the dinnerware is elegant, yet not too formal: Napkins of various colors dress up the place settings. Gold charger plates add elegance to each setting in the makeover space, and blue and white napkin rings provide continuity with the Asian-style porcelain present throughout the space. Because the table in the inspiration room was larger than the table in the makeover space, additional accessories—such as tall candlesticks—are present; by paring back the elements on the makeover table, the look is clean rather than cluttered, which is perfect for a formal setting.

The Look for Less

When you have an unlimited decorating budget, the sky's the limit: You can afford one-of-a-kind pieces and authentic antiques and artifacts. But if your budget is more down-to-earth, consider these tips before you begin your next room redo.

▶ **Be willing to paint your own walls, which allows you to "play" with colors and decorative treatments.** "If you make a mistake," Jen Jordan says, "you can always cover it and try again." Jen sketched the acanthus scrolls in this room freehand; however, she says stenciling a large-scale repeat pattern would have the same effect.

▶ **For a formal look draperies should hang to the floor or gather in a puddle.** To avoid hemming cut the panels extra-long, then tuck under the raw edges.

▶ **Dining room furniture can be expensive.** Emulate the look of a china cabinet by coordinating mismatched top and bottom pieces, which you can find in hotel liquidation sales, consignment stores, and almost any furniture showroom. Make sure the wood finishes are compatible, Jen advises, although it doesn't matter if the colors aren't exact. Formal styles typically dictate dark woods such as mahogany or cherry; country looks use lighter woods.

▶ **Store-bought blue and white pieces make the pottery in the Sensibly Chic room look like a museum collection, but you can use your own china just as effectively.** Group pieces of similar colors and varied shapes, or arrange many different pieces for more eclectic appeal.

▶ **Save a lot on a high-quality chandelier by purchasing a nonfunctioning one from an antique store, flea market, or estate sale.** As long as the fixture was once electrical, you can rewire it for relatively little cost using a kit available at home centers.

▶ **Although they are usually more expensive than square or oblong tables, round tables are worth the investment for the intimacy and comfort they afford.** Many showrooms do not readily show round tables, so be sure to ask.

makeover room $1,880

Lesson Nine Creating Focal Points

Focal points draw the eye and unify all the elements in a room. This may be a furnishing, an architectural element (such as a large picture window or a fireplace), or a stunning piece of artwork. In these guest bedrooms dramatic floor-to-ceiling window treatments, warm colors, and rich textures draw attention to the centers of interest: a fabric-encased bed and a distinguished marble writing desk. The expensive original—the "Golden Gate Bedroom"—is aptly named for its view of San Francisco's Golden Gate Bridge. Although the view from the Sensibly Chic space may not be as impressive, the use of size, color, and texture helps to create an alluring setting almost as dramatic as the inspiration room— for thousands less. If you desire a bedroom that is romantic and inviting— and a landmark of good design—look to these spaces for motivation.

	Sensible Makeover	Inspiration
Wall Paint	$130	$1,200
Window Treatments/ Hardware	$375	$2,900
Bed Frame	$258	$2,100
Coverlet/Pillows	$230	$2,850
Dresser	$250	$3,600
Bronze Statue	$20	$6,000
Prints	$123	$975
Desk/Chair	$274	$4,800
Desk Lamp/ Accessories	$125	$850
Rug	$75	$5,200
Sconce Shades	$20	*
TOTAL	$1,880	$30,475

*The inspiration room did not have wall sconces, but the existing sconces in the makeover room are retained.

Cushion a Corner Focal-point furnishings are typically placed at the center of a room— a dining table in the middle of the floor or a sofa centered against a wall. But both these rooms successfully break the rules. According to inspiration room designer Jeanese Rowell, "We tried to make the room multifaceted with combination sleeping, working, and sitting areas." Jeanese pushed the bed into the corner, adding height and textures to establish its importance,

A combination of sleeping and sitting/working areas makes these guest rooms as functional as they are beautiful. Dark wood tones, luxurious drapes, and warm color on the walls make the spaces feel enclosed and comfortable. Custom and antique furnishings and accessories put the price tag of the inspiration room right at more than $30,000; however, by following the design strategies of the original, the Sensible Chic team created a comparable space left for less than $2,000.

inspiration room $30,475

▶ For a video demonstration for creating the headboard and footboard, visit HGTV.com/sensiblechic

and concurrently leaving ample room for a desk and seating.

"The bed sets the tone of the room as an escape," Jeanese explains. Wrapped in custom-made fabric and a cherrywood frame, the inspiration bed is welcoming and warm. A tone-on-tone silk coverlet with a diamond motif contrasts against the rust-color walls, while layers of hand-sewn pillows add splashes of color that attract the eye—all pushing the bed to focal-point status.

The makeover bed is equally inviting, with a quilted cotton coverlet in a square motif and creamy buff color that's paired with a khaki-color dust ruffle. "It has the same tailored look as the inspiration bed," *Sensible Chic*'s Jen Jordan explains. In place of the expensive custom-made upholstered frame, Jen scaled back to a fabric-covered headboard and footboard, which still create a feeling of enclosure. A pile of plush pillows, although substantially

"This room is all about the bed," Jen Jordan says. Floor-to-ceiling drapes, an upholstered headboard and footboard, and plush pillows draw the eye to the romantic corner above—which closely mimics the opulent look of the inspiration room right. The deep rust wall color and a shaded sconce add warmth and depth to the Sensibly Chic space.

less expensive, emulates the opulent appeal of the inspiration room, welcoming guests to relax.

To emphasize the focal-point corner even more, gold-color silk taffeta draperies hang from ceiling rods in the inspiration room, wrapping around the bed like a canopy. The rich texture, height, and color of these treatments create drama as well as intimacy. In the makeover room fragile ceilings with cracking plaster prevented the *Sensible Chic* team from hanging anything. Instead Jen draped synthetic acetate taffeta—with a similar feel and sheen as the natural silk but costing just a fraction of the original—from floor to ceiling on two walls to give the space a sense of privacy.

The final piece of the focal-point puzzle is the wall color, which brings even more attention to the bed in each space. In the inspiration room a rust wall color, which echoes the Golden Gate Bridge outside, is chosen; this warm color communicates romance and allows the light-color bed to have even more prominence. Dramatic moldings painted in a crisp white add architectural detail and a sense of formality.

To echo the original room, the *Sensible Chic* team also chose a warm rust hue for the walls, but instead of using this color to reach the ceiling, the existing molding —that divides the upper quarter of the wall from the lower three-quarters—acts as a buffer in the tall room. By painting only the space below the molding, a sense of intimacy is created; painting the upper portion of the wall and ceiling a light beige softens the walls and isn't as stark as white would be.

Picture Perfect

Framed artwork may be used in any room in the home to add interest to walls and continue a design theme. Here are some hints for selecting the perfect frames and mats and for arranging your pieces in an artful way:

- **Find the perfect frame.** Look for the most substantial frame that you can afford, but select a frame that suits the print or photograph and fits the style of the room where you will display the piece. For instance, the complementary gold frames in these rooms speak to a sophisticated, traditional style. For a more modern look, black frames with white mats would be appropriate.

- **Do it yourself.** Discount framing shops, crafts stores, and mass merchandisers offer inexpensive frames without glass; purchase the glass separately at a hardware or framing shop and back the frame yourself with foam-core board.

- **Match the mat.** Whether you are framing paintings, photographs, renderings, or illustrations, a mat makes artwork appear more valuable, even if it's not. Precut mats are widely available at crafts and art supply stores. Generally, white and cream may be your best bets to complement the light hues in a room. If you desire a colored mat, choose one that complements both the artwork and the wall color.

- **Experiment with picture groupings.** According to Jen Jordan, there is no rule of thumb concerning how artwork should be displayed, but some arrangements work best for some decorating styles. A symmetrical grouping—pictures hung in a straight horizontal or vertical row or an even-number grouping—works well in a more formal space, while an asymmetrical, uneven arrangement can be stimulating and keeps the eye moving in a more casual setting.

- **Play with placement to avoid unsightly holes in the wall.** Cut out pieces of paper the same size as the pictures you intend to hang. Tape the cut paper shapes to the wall in different arrangements using low-tack painter's tape. Evaluate how the arrangement works in relation to the other elements in the room. Once you like the arrangement, nail picture hangers to the wall through the paper, tear the paper away, and hang the pictures.

Antique prints of San Francisco sights in the makeover room *left* echo the view of the Golden Gate Bridge from the inspiration room. To add more importance to the desk, Jen hand-painted a box to look like a Chinese treasure and added picture frames to personalize the space.

Maintaining Balance Although the bed is the place of emphasis in each room, a dresser is still key in balancing weight in the space—and it offers guests a place to store clothing and personal items. The tapered cherrywood chest of drawers that proudly stands in the inspiration room provides perfect balance because of its size and scale. In the makeover room Jen looked for something with the same height and modern style. Although she was unable to find a tapered counterpart, her dresser of choice in a dark wood finish still fits the bill: By changing the drawer pulls on the less expensive option, she accomplished a similar look for thousands less.

A contemporary bronze statue and framed antique prints—all depicting San Francisco landmarks—also add interest and importance to the dresser in each room. Coordinating gold frames speak to the luxurious tones in the rooms. Jen found landmark scenes similar to those displayed in the inspiration room, but suggests that the images could be anything. "The idea here was for them to look vintage," she says, but family photos or sports scenes would work just as well if you enjoy them.

The most important consideration in choosing the focal-point arrangement for this wall was selecting coordinating frames and mats that make the prints feel like a cohesive unit.

Write Home About It The desk is another place of emphasis in the inspiration room, calling attention to itself with a cherrywood base and magnificent terra-cotta marble top. "I chose the top because of the color," Jeanese explains, "and because I wanted to add another material that had some sheen to it." She also made the piece more versatile by creating modular pedestals. The top can be dismantled, and the side pieces used as nightstands if desired. A chair covered in luxurious mohair upholstery accompanies the multipurpose desk and offers a restful spot for anyone who needs to jot a note or change footwear.

Because the makeover budget couldn't support an extravagance like marble, Jen created a striking substitute. She found an inexpensive walnut desk and created a faux marble effect with paint. Although this version cannot be dismantled, the size and style of the piece still establish a strong presence. An upholstered parsons

chair, which Jen found affordably at a discount furniture store, adds comfortable seating at the desk. Its chenille upholstery resembles the expensive designer chair, and the color blends perfectly with the neutral-tone bedding—unifying these focal-point features.

The desk accessories add interest and complete the arrangement, though Jeanese says they're one of the hardest parts of design. She chose an inlaid lacquered Chinese box, some books, a tall candelabra, and a sleek black and gold lamp for the desk. "Sometimes you just pick up things and make them work," she says. "The small details are the ones you have a tendency to notice because of their importance in maintaining the theme."

The contemporary bronze statue that stands on top of the tapered cherrywood dresser in the inspiration room above cost a whopping $6,000. The wood statue opposite has graceful lines that mimic the original, but it cost just $20. A coat of paint helps the piece appear more expensive than it is.

Jen could not afford a marble-top desk, so she faux-painted the top on a less expensive wood piece. The tall candelabra and desk lamp with a black shade add height and classic formality.

The Look for Less

Adding a sense of high-cost luxury to any room in your home can be accomplished on a budget. Use these tips to help you create the room of your dreams for minimal expense.

▶ **To soften your bed without the expense of an upholstered frame, create your own upholstered headboard and/or footboard.** For the Sensibly Chic space Jen Jordan cut plywood shapes, covered them with foam, then stitched slipcovers to fit snugly over the plywood shapes.

▶ **Layer plush pillows on top of affordable linens to establish a luxurious look in your bedroom.** Different shapes, textures, and colors of pillows add interest and comfort to the most important feature of any bedroom: the bed.

▶ **Though they are small details, hardware for doors and case goods can make a big difference in conveying a style; think of it as jewelry for your cabinets and furnishings.** Jen changed the handles on the dresser she chose to resemble the classic lines of the stately piece in the inspiration room. Look to home improvement centers for a wide variety of styles that will suit your decor.

▶ **Because a marble top was not realistic for the *Sensible Chic* team's budget, Jen painted a faux marble finish on a less expensive desk for impressive results.** Before committing time and energy to painting a piece, look in books, take classes, and practice on sample boards, Jen suggests. Then you'll feel more confident with the faux marbling technique.

▶ **Add romantic presence with a candelabra.** Choose its size and the height of its candles depending on the scale of the room and how much prominence you want the piece to have (for instance, tall ceilings suggest a tall candelabra). In the case of the makeover space, extra-tall candles make the candelabra more imposing and draw the eye up on a parallel with the bed curtains.

Jen saved hundreds of dollars on accessories by shopping at discount stores and outlets. "Products are much more plentiful from all over the world [at these places]," she says. The five-arm gold candelabra is a key element that sets the rich tone of the room. Inserting tall candles and positioning it on a stack of books raises the candelabra to a level of importance—making it a mini-focal point on the desk. To re-create the inlaid Chinese box, Jen painted an ordinary jewelry box and added stenciled detail in a golden color, achieving an elaborate look.

To bridge the gap between the two distinct areas in the room, Jeanese chose a silk and wool Tibetan rug. Placed on a diagonal, the large rug helps to define each area and adds a sense of luxury underfoot. Jen found a low-pile area rug with a taupe border for the Sensibly Chic space. The colors and size of the low-cost version have the same welcoming effect, while connecting the living areas.

makeover room $2,444

Lesson Ten Don't Forget the Fun

Oversize furniture and amusing accessories entertain a guise of whimsy—and offer all kinds of surprises. In these rooms swirls, checkerboards, large clocks, sunny colors, and overstuffed chairs are reminiscent of Alice in Wonderland—but these living rooms tell their own story. The large-scale furnishings in the inspiration room are in sync with their natural surroundings: giant California redwood trees. According to inspiration room designer Linda Applewhite, fun objects, interesting patterns, and juxtaposed elements all work together to create a whimsical feel. Yet with a price tag of more than $60,000, the cost of this lighthearted look is not so whimsical. The *Sensible Chic* team, led by makeover designer Jen Jordan, shows that fun can be just as accessible for tens of thousands less.

Set the Surround With 13-foot-high ceilings and 9-foot-high windows, the oversize architecture of the inspiration room lends itself to sizable style. Hand-plastered walls in a golden tone create a feeling of intimacy despite the large proportions of the space. In the makeover room Jen painted the walls with a golden apricot colorwash. This easy-to-do technique provides visual texture and dimension

	Sensible Makeover	Inspiration
Wall Plaster/Paint	$85	$12,000
Built-In Cabinetry	$209	$8,000
Garden Urns	$111	$3,000
Clock	$280	$3,900
Chairs/Pillows	$438	$6,120
Accent Tables	$200	$3,680
Frog Statue	$15	$160
Rug	$108	$7,050
Coffee Table/Bowl	$114	$3,730
Sofa/Throw/Pillows	$742	$9,300
Fireplace Mantel	*	$2,350
Mantel Art/Topiaries	$142	$1,190
Firewood Holder	**	$300
TOTAL	$2,444	$60,780

*The fireplace mantel in the inspiration room is made of faux-painted wood, antique iron corbels, and dentil molding. Because the makeover room has an existing mantel, this is not a makeover room expense.

**The makeover room has a nonworking fireplace, so it did not require a log holder.

inspiration room $60,780

Sometimes it's the unexpected—in size, shape, and color—that makes a room work. With large-scale furnishings, an oversize antique clock, lots of fun shapes, and happy colors, each of these living rooms appears larger than life. While the custom-designed inspiration room left cost a whopping $60,780, the makeover space opposite was created for a mere $2,444—but it doesn't skimp on whimsical style.

If you want an aged, worn look for the accents in your room, but you don't want to invest in antiques with authentic patina, look no further than this crafty solution: A combination of paint, sand, and moss makes the low-cost garden finials in the Sensibly Chic space resemble the iron topiary planters in the inspiration room.

ONE: Either purchase a pretinted glazing medium or mix 2 parts glazing medium to 1 part acrylic paint. **Note:** To achieve an old, worn appearance, choose a dark color, such as black, as was used for this example. Using a paintbrush, randomly apply the glazing medium or glaze/paint mixture onto the decorative accent; let dry.

TWO: Pour about 1 inch of sand into a shallow container with sides. Apply spray adhesive to the entire accent piece; immediately roll the piece in the sand, completely coating it. Wipe off any excess sand.

THREE: Using a hot-glue gun, apply crafts moss in the crevices of the base to resemble natural moss growth; let dry.

FOUR: To further age the accent piece, lightly dab on a highlight color (such as gold or light green); let dry.

to the walls for a fraction of the cost of the custom plaster treatment.

"This room is very much about connecting indoors and out," Linda says, which explains the mantel decor of antique iron topiary planters and an original floral painting on ground steel canvas. Jen planted similar garden motifs on the existing mantel in the Sensibly Chic space. She fashioned her own pair of topiaries with plastic-foam balls, moss, and a hot-glue gun. She also embellished an inexpensive store-bought poster with gel medium to create the illusion of an expensive piece of art.

On the floor of the inspiration room, Linda added a handwoven Tibetan wool area rug that firmly establishes the capricious tone. "We play with it by sprinkling blue and red dots all over," she says. The rug covers a checkerboard floor, which complements other checked motifs in the room. Jen's variation has large random swirls that speak to the same frivolity. Low-contrast, light tones on the floors make each room feel larger.

A casual arrangement of fresh flowers adds to the lighthearted tone of the makeover space. Oversize swirls on the sisal rug bring movement and fun pattern underfoot; the rug anchors the conversation area for a pulled-together look.

Climb the Walls To complement the large features in the inspiration room, oversize accessories were a must. To balance the height of the windows and transoms, Linda designed tall checkerboard wall units that repeat the checkerboard pattern in the floor. These matching units flank the focal-point mantel in dramatic style. The cabinet detail is also noteworthy: dentil molding along the top and iron swirls for door hardware. "Good design repeats itself," Linda says. In the inspiration room, dentil molding also trims the fireplace, checkerboards cover the chairs, and swirls appear in the fireplace screen. Linda also added antique iron corbels to reiterate the garden theme.

In the makeover room the *Sensible Chic* team made the checkerboard cabinets from plywood that is faux-finished and trimmed to resemble the original units. "When you see the checkerboard in the room," Jen says, "you immediately know it's fun." She also added "homegrown" finials made from plaster castings that she aged with black-tinted glaze, rolled in sand, and highlighted with crafts moss and light-color paint.

Another key to creating whimsy is juxtaposing old with new. In this case a turn-of-the-century French clock—once used in a train station—surprises the eye not only by its size, but also by its obvious placement in the high-price space. "There are a lot of layers

Out on a Whim

Because the look is creative, unexpected, and full of fun, a whimsical room is one of the easiest styles to accomplish on a budget. However, although the look is casual, it must look pulled-together to be chic. Follow these cues to create a not-too-serious look in any room in your home:

- **Mix happy colors.** Choose a bright palette of similar values. In these rooms golden apricot, strawberry red, and lime green accents offer a balanced mix of warm and cool colors.

- **Juxtapose elements: large and small, antique and contemporary, country and formal.** By playing with contrast you can create a fun, unfussy look. For instance the overscale clock contrasts with the tiny checkerboard upholstery on the chairs below. The weathered topiaries are striking against the clean-line contemporary furnishings.

- **Incorporate large-scale elements.** Even a single oversize object, such as the railroad clock, can set a happy tone for the whole room by being an instant conversation starter.

- **Choose whimsical shapes.** Introduce funky patterns like swirls, checks, circles, and stripes on the furniture, window treatments, and floor. Also seek out playful accents, such as the ceramic frog in the Sensibly Chic space.

▶ For a video demonstration of the cabinet project, visit HGTV.com/sensiblechic

juxtaposed," Linda explains. "Indoors and outdoors, new and old, unexpected sizes and shapes." Although Jen was limited by a smaller space, she succeeded in creating the same surprising feel with a large clock. She suggests searching the Internet or mail-order catalogs for French reproduction clocks, which are widely available and much more affordable than original antiques.

Fall into the Furniture To complement the antique patina of the accessories, contemporary chairs speak to ultimate comfort with their plump, oversize

styling. In the inspiration room two chairs with black and white checkerboard upholstery create one side of the cozy conversation area. The chairs—topped with pillows in vivid warm hues—offer a comfy place to read or visit with family or friends. But at a price of more than $6,000 the chairs alone equal nearly three times the price of the entire makeover room! For an inexpensive—but just as inviting—sitting area, Jen reinvigorated chairs purchased at a hotel liquidator using fitted sage- and cream-color checked slipcovers. Rust-color cording, which offers a warm contrast to the slipcovers, emulates the original trim.

The inspiration room sofa is similarly big and bold in a happy raspberry red that relates to the red in the chairs. For the makeover Jen chose 8 yards of upholstery-grade damask to cover the store-bought sofa seat cushions; a faux suede fabric covers the rest of the couch. "It was a great way to get a custom look for not a lot of money," Jen says. She also removed the sofa legs to level the seating. Store-bought and handmade pillows repeat the colors present throughout the space: Florals and pin dot patterns add to the whimsy, and fringe and tassels add a playful element. "A geometric throw over the sofa back is another way of saying, 'Make yourself at home'," Jen says.

Nine separate cubbies, some with cabinet doors, create a playful checkerboard effect left. Chairs slipcovered in a checkerboard-print fabric and trimmed in red piping and golden-color polka-dot pillows echo the painted tones of the cabinet.

The oversize clock right—which resembles the expensive antique in the inspiration room—immediately conveys a sense of humor.

The "hippo table," named for its chunky legs, is another custom-made whimsical element in the inspiration room. Because such an unusual table is hard to find, Jen opted to stay simple with a maple surface and bowed sides. "It couldn't be a petite Victorian table," she says. "It's important that it be a bright color and match the scale and whimsical theme of the room."

Finally side tables add anchor points with their dark tones and geometric shapes.

"They let you know where things are starting and stopping," Jen says. Although the tables in the inspiration room were round, Jen found comparable square alternatives that double as both display space and seating. A ceramic frog completes the room—a small but engaging jovial detail.

With its larger-than-life appeal and mix of juxtaposed elements, each of these rooms is a lesson in fun and surprise. "Do it wherever you can," Linda advises. Even just one unexpected element can turn a room from blah to boisterous. "Don't we need more to smile at these days?"

Jen mixed pin dots and geometric patterns right to mimic the pillows in the inspiration room above. An upholstery-grade fabric with swirls on a checkerboard background covers the sofa cushions and repeats other whimsical shapes in the room right.

Juxtaposing old and new, light and dark creates an element of surprise. Dark-stained side tables below help ground the room and offer contrast against the light wood coffee table and cabinet unit. The ceramic frog adds to the unexpected in this fun space.

The Look for Less

Are you looking for an inexpensive way to decorate your home—but not skimp on style? Check out these great ideas to dress up your home whatever your budget.

▶ **Achieve a fantasy look on the walls, even if you're an amateur painter.** Mix a colorwash of 4 parts glazing medium to 1 part paint. Dip a brush in the mixture and apply the paint in a crosshatching motion.

▶ **Large-scale, overstuffed furniture tends to be expensive.** If your budget is limited, look for pieces that are as plump and comfortable as possible. The *Sensible Chic* team couldn't afford to buy new, so Jen Jordan stitched slipcovers for chairs purchased at a hotel liquidation store. She also supplied her own funky fabric to cover the seat cushions of a store bought couch.

▶ **Repeat patterns to unify elements.** Squares in the cabinetry repeat themselves on the sofa cushions and again on the side tables. Swirls in the rug repeat the circular movement of the clock and topiaries.

▶ **The *Sensible Chic* team built the cabinet affordably from a 4-foot-square plywood box, divided into nine equal sections.** If you aren't a skilled builder, you can find similar bookcases at furniture stores and mass merchandisers. Stow books and living room essentials in the closed cabinets, and use the open shelves to display a favorite collection. Shop flea markets and garage sales for items, such as old garden finials, antique yarn spools, or old wood bowling pins to create the lighthearted look seen in the Sensibly Chic space.

▶ **Fresh flowers are appropriate for a whimsical look.** "They make your life seem beautiful," Jen says. Also accessorize with arrangements of fresh fruit that add color and natural scents.

Ser

Know Your Style

Close your eyes and think about your dream home. Is it filled with priceless antiques, tailored fabrics, and ornate furnishings perfect for hosting formal gatherings? Or is the atmosphere more relaxed, with a focus on comfort, soothing colors, and well-worn treasures? Now open your eyes and look around you: Is your home an accurate portrayal of who you are—and what you want your surroundings to be? Even if your budget is tight, you can make your house a place you love to come home to.

This section begins with a fun-to-answer quiz, designed to help you identify the style of decorating that best reflects your personality, attitudes, and interests. Following the quiz you will explore each style in depth: You will learn all about the colors, textures, surfaces, and furnishings that best characterize each style to guide you on your next decorating adventure.

What's Your Style?

Decorating is all about creating spaces that accurately reflect who you are. When you identify what makes a home welcoming, relaxing, and nurturing, you will be well on your way to letting your true personality shine. That's what this quiz is all about: helping you acknowledge your preferences and then give you the tools to make your decorating dreams a reality. For each question select the answer that best describes your taste; if none are exactly accurate, choose the answer that is closest. Then, turn to page 99 to analyze your results.

ONE For you, the perfect vacation would be:

a. Touring England's stately homes
b. A weekend in New York City
c. Exploring the Great Wall of China
d. Fishing, boating, or hiking in Maine
e. A month-long stay at the Ritz in Paris

TWO If money were no object, which of these artists' work would you display in your home?

a. Monet
b. Andy Warhol
c. Gauguin
d. Grandma Moses
e. Cecil Beaton

THREE Your ideal dining experience is:

a. A black-tie, four-course dinner at the White House
b. Take out
c. A luau complete with tiki torches and pupu platters
d. A backyard barbecue with friends
e. A late-night dinner at the trendiest restaurant in town

FOUR If you could move into the set of any movie, it would be:

a. A stately country manor like the one shown in *Remains of the Day*
b. Rock Hudson's apartment in *Pillow Talk*
c. The Chinese Imperial Palace as depicted in *The Last Emperor*
d. Francesca's farmhouse in *The Bridges of Madison County*
e. Nick and Nora Charles' penthouse apartment in *The Thin Man*

FIVE The one accessory that you can't leave home without is:

a. An Hermés scarf
b. The latest cell phone
c. A red coral necklace
d. A monogrammed L.L. Bean tote bag
e. A Kate Spade bag

SIX You're inspired to redecorate after watching:

a. *A Room with a View*
b. *2001: A Space Odyssey*
c. *Out of Africa*
d. *Babe*
e. *Breakfast at Tiffany's*

SEVEN You feel most at home in a room with walls that are:

a. Paneled with rich walnut wood
b. Painted stark white
c. Lacquered red
d. Covered in a cabbage rose print
e. Mirrored á la the bedroom of Marlene Dietrich

EIGHT You like to spend your Saturday afternoons:

a. Hosting a tea party for friends
b. Touring local art galleries
c. Exploring new parts of town
d. Working in your garden
e. Pampering yourself at a local spa

NINE For a special dinner party, you create a centerpiece using:

a. Several dozen roses in a large silver bowl
b. A stainless-steel trough filled with succulents and moss
c. Orchids floating in a lacquered bowl
d. Primroses planted in painted pots
e. A bouquet of pink peonies

TEN You're planning to re-cover your favorite sofa, and you are drawn to:

a. Toile
b. Leather
c. Silk
d. Denim
e. Damask

ELEVEN Your signature scent is:

a. Polo Sport by Ralph Lauren
b. Obsession by Calvin Klein
c. Opium
d. Romance by Ralph Lauren
e. Chanel No. 5

TWELVE For you, the perfect place to take a nap would be:

a. A four-poster bed with tailored bedding
b. A lounge chair in front of the TV
c. A daybed draped in netting
d. A hammock in the garden
e. First-class on a flight to Europe

THIRTEEN You may not be a collector, but you can't resist:

a. 18th- and 19th-century portraits
b. Furnishings from the 1950s and 1960s
c. Asian porcelain of any kind
d. Botanical prints in weathered wood frames
e. Anything French

FOURTEEN The colors you love to live with come from:

a. The interiors of historical homes
b. Modern works of art
c. Faraway places like India and Asia
d. Nature
e. Hollywood movies of the 1950s

FIFTEEN When you sit down to read the paper, you like to sink into:

a. A tailored wingback chair with an ottoman
b. A black leather club chair
c. A pile of pillows on the floor
d. Grandma's old rocking chair
e. A leopard-print chaise lounge

SIXTEEN Your dream kitchen is:

a. A sophisticated space with furniture-style cabinets and a butler's pantry
b. A room with stainless-steel cabinets that is open to a central dining space
c. A room that has been laid out using the principles of *feng shui*
d. A cozy space with painted cabinets, well-worn wood floors, and an antique stove
e. A galley with folding doors

SEVENTEEN If you could add one thing to your home, it would be:

a. A formal fireplace with a fancy marble mantel
b. A wall of windows
c. Sliding doors made from lattice screens
d. A picket fence in the front yard
e. A spa-style bath with a sauna and steam shower

EIGHTEEN Fabrics that you're drawn to include:

a. Stripes, plaids, and checks
b. Solid colors
c. Batiks, silks, and linens
d. Florals
e. Animal patterns and Pucci-inspired prints

NINETEEN If you had a fireplace mantel, you would display:

a. A selection of blue-and-white porcelain
b. A sculpture by your favorite contemporary artist
c. A collection of seashells and coral
d. A vase filled with flowers picked from your garden
e. An eclectic arrangement of family photographs and vintage silver pieces

TWENTY In your dream house, your bedroom window frames views of:

a. A boxwood maze
b. A city skyline
c. A tropical rain forest
d. A meadow filled with wildflowers
e. The Eiffel Tower

Evaluating the Results

Tally the number of times you answered a, b, c, d, or e. The letter you chose most frequently indicates the decorating style you are drawn to.

a. Traditional Your look is clearly classic—inspired by historic homes from Charleston to Williamsburg. Key ingredients include Chippendale, Queen Anne, or Empire-style tables, chairs, cabinets, and sofas made from rich woods like cherry or mahogany. If you had your druthers, you would move to England and take up residence on a classic country estate. For you, family heirlooms and antiques define comfort. Classic color schemes include blue and white as well as yellow with dashes of pink and green.

▸ For additional information on all these decorating styles—and more—visit HGTV.com/designstyles

b. Contemporary Sleek lines and simple profiles are two hallmarks of this sophisticated style. Others include carefully edited surroundings and open interiors. Color is kept to a minimum, with white (and varying shades thereof) winning the popular vote. To break up the white, you like to cover your walls with important photographs and simple, but sophisticated, paintings and prints. Furniture tends to be functional (think Scandinavian and Italian designs), and every piece has a dedicated purpose—after all, you like clutter to be kept to a minimum.

c. Exotic or Ethnic Your home may be in New Hampshire, but your heart is in Hong Kong. You crave stylishly cluttered spaces that overflow with collections culled from all the exotic places you have traveled—a selection of silk wall hangings, or a grouping of porcelain bowls and vases—or purchased at a local import store. When it comes to choosing colors, you lean toward spicy, sophisticated hues, such as reds, yellows, and oranges.

d. Country or Cottage You crave comfortable, well-worn spaces with timeless appeal. You prefer furnishings that aren't fussy, like a sofa slipcovered in denim or a table painted a cheery hue. Relaxed room arrangements are key, with plenty of places to put your feet. Your preferred color palette includes the tried-and-true (think red, white, and blue), as well as a host of hues inspired by nature.

e. Chic You've got style, and you like to show it. You wear the latest fashions and you expect your home to follow suit. Your furnishings, like your wardrobe, are a mix of classic staples (a simple sofa that can be re-covered on a whim) and showstopping accents, like the latest must-have lamp or electronic gadget—all with a dollop of sleek Hollywood glamour. When it comes to color, you take your cues from the runway, selecting hues that reflect current fashion trends. You're inspired by current design trends from cosmopolitan cities like Paris, London, Milan, and New York. Above all else you choose accent pieces wisely, selecting things like pillows and throws that can easily be changed out at a moment's notice.

TRADITIONAL

If you love interiors that are refined—complete with authentic (or reproduction) 18th-century furnishings, tailored window treatments, and fine accessories such as pillows made of luxurious fabrics and silver candlesticks—you no doubt long for a space steeped in traditional elegance.

Although true-blue traditional style may be rich with high-price furnishings and accessories, it is possible to achieve a classic look for less. If authentic antiques—which can cost tens of thousands of dollars at auctions and antiques stores—are out of your reach, look for pieces with the hallmarks of these classic furnishings in consignment shops, at flea markets, and even at mass merchandisers and chain furniture stores. Similarly, you may find lush Oriental-style rugs at home centers and mass merchandisers, offering bold pattern and color for the floor at a fraction of the cost of an antique. Accessories and artwork perfect for this enduring style are readily available at these same outlets, as well as import stores (where you will find inexpensive porcelain in blue and white) and secondhand stores (where you may find prints and paintings for a steal).

Furnishings

Finely crafted furnishings from Europe and America—typically made of high-quality hardwoods—are the hallmark of traditional style. Upholstered pieces, such as benches and reading chairs, are designed for

FURNISHINGS	Chippendale, Queen Anne, or Empire-style furnishings made from rich woods, including cherry and mahogany, are typical of traditional-style interiors. Upholstered pieces such as benches, wing and club chairs, and ottomans have a tailored look. All furnishings typically have a mix of straight and curved lines.
COLORS	Classic colors include neutrals, such as gray, beige, and white, as well as very dark and light tones of nearly every color in the spectrum—from deep reds, blues, and greens to pastels derived from nature.
FABRICS	Lavish patterns in large florals, scenic toile de Jouy, crisp stripes, and tone-on-tone prints are hallmarks of this style.
WINDOW TREATMENTS	Vertical and horizontal blinds and full draperies made of rich fabrics are typical of traditional spaces. Common window treatment fabric patterns include plaids, stripes, and florals. Cornices and valances may top the treatment.
FLOOR COVERINGS	Hardwood floors—or neutral-color carpeting—are often covered with large, beautiful Oriental-style rugs.
LIGHTING	Lamps with delicate silk shades in neutral hues and lights that resemble candles are commonly seen in traditional spaces.
ACCESSORIES	Decorate a traditional space with fine porcelain pieces, embroidered or crewelwork pillows, prints of botanicals and landscapes, and grandfather clocks. Mirrors often have gilded or ornately detailed wood frames.
OTHER CHARACTERISTICS	Furnishings and accessories are often symmetrically arranged for a sense of formality. Traditional spaces should remain uncluttered. Crown molding is a common element of traditional rooms—often painted in a crisp white.

Complete with rich upholstery, silk throw pillows, and softly curved lines, the sofa above left looks inviting. All these elements contribute to traditional styling.

The sitting room left is a perfect example of a traditional space: sumptuous silk upholstery, gilded-frame mirrors, perfectly symmetrical tables and lamps on either side of an upholstered sofa, a balanced grouping of framed prints (reflected in the mirror), and decorative elements such as a bouquet of white roses.

Covered in pampering pink and white upholstery, this chair above exhibits traditional styling, with its tailored look and softly curved lines.

Sensibly Traditional

For a dining room that's truly traditional, see pages 70–77. The brightly colored Oriental-style rug, dark-stained furnishings, and blue and white porcelain pieces exhibit the hallmarks of traditional style.

comfort and often have tailored details, including crisp pleats and button tufts. Overall traditional-style furnishings incorporate a combination of straight and gently curved lines.

Colors

Traditional spaces can be bathed in nearly any color, including neutrals, deep bold hues, and pretty pastels. You may introduce these colors by way of fabrics used as pillows and window treatments, area rugs, furniture upholstery, and even opulent wall coverings (such as embossed wallpapers or wallcoverings with floral or strong geometric patterns).

Fabrics

High-quality fabrics—such as silks, velvets, and damask—are often in solid colors or depict florals of various sizes. Plaids, stripes, paisley, and toile de Jouy are motifs commonly seen in traditional-style interiors. Fabrics lend themselves to tailored window treatments, pillows, and upholstery.

Window Treatments

In a traditional space, windows are dressed in formal treatments, such as tailored Roman shades, crisp pleated panels, and loosely draped swags. Draperies are often floor length and trimmed with tassels and fringe. They can hang from ornate

The dining room above left is traditional elegance at its best. The combination of luxurious raw silk window treatments and a perfectly symmetrical arrangement of accessories and dinnerware on the table speaks to the formality of the style.

The chairs above incorporate both gently curved shapes—in the harp detail and arched arms—and straight lines. The two chairs sit on either side of a small table; they are in perfect symmetry (a hallmark of traditional style).

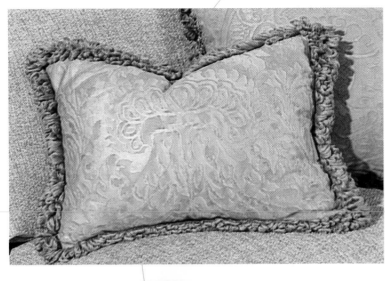

Expensive Fortuney fabric—handmade in Italy—adds a sense of opulence to the sofa left. Showcasing a high-cost fabric as a pillow makes it an instant focal point—and is a wise investment because only a small amount of fabric is needed.

The lamp below is a nice companion to a formal space: Its brass base has some elegant details, and the simple silk shade is a quiet nod to formality.

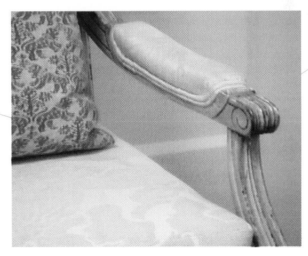

Piles of pillows of different shapes and sizes and in luxurious white and blue silk fabrics are an inviting touch on a bed with an ornately carved antique headboard above.

The chair right—with upholstery in a soft pink print and delicately scrolled details on the arm—is a shining example of a furnishing suited for a room decorated in a traditional style.

The ornately framed mirror above is a perfect accent for a traditional-style room.

The opulent wall sconce above right—complete with candles for an intimate glow—is a fitting companion for a traditional room. The raw silk swag that dresses a neighboring window is casually draped over a simple finial, ushering in a relaxed feel to the formal space.

A large antique rug right—with rich blues and reds in a bold pattern—is just right for this traditionally styled living room. It adds a jolt of color to a mostly neutral space and warms the hardwood floor.

rods with decorative finials to enhance the elegant effect. Valances and cornice boxes covered in coordinating fabrics can top traditional-style panels and high-quality vertical blinds or they may be used alone. Both valances and cornice boxes may have shaped edges—scallops, scrolls, or geometric designs—to add soft architectural interest to a window.

Floor Coverings

Hardwood floors look right at home in traditional spaces, as do neutral-tone carpets that don't call too much attention to themselves. To warm up a traditional space—and add some rich color and pattern to a floor—you can incorporate large Oriental-style area rugs, from fine antiques to reproduction floor coverings.

Lighting

Light fixtures—table and floor lamps, sconces, and chandeliers—for traditional spaces may take a number of forms. Elaborate and ornate fixtures, with details like scrolls and flowers, work well, as do simple and stately designs, such as a classic urn shape for a lamp base. Lamp bases and sconces are often made of pewter or brass; chandeliers may also be made of metal, but the addition of crystals enhances a formal feel. Lampshades are typically made of high-quality materials, including silk, in neutral tones or dark hues.

Accessories

Walls and tabletops alike offer spaces to display traditional-style accessories. The key to accessorizing a traditional space is symmetry: Like furnishings, decorative elements should balance one another and appear uncluttered. Hang prints symmetrically and use decorative accessories in pairs to emphasize balance.

On walls, landscapes, portraits, and botanicals make handsome additions to a traditional room—as do elegant tapestries. Mirrors in gilded or highly detailed wood frames are commonly seen in traditional spaces.

Tabletop pieces for traditionally styled living rooms and bedrooms often include porcelain and china, silver trays and serving pieces, lush floral arrangements, candlesticks, and leather-bound books. For a traditional dining space, china with either a delicate floral motif or a simple gold rim, stemware made of delicate handblown glass or crystal, and brightly polished silver are nice companions.

A small antique clock, such as the one above, is a classic accent for a tabletop in a traditional space. Its ornate details mimic many traditional-style furnishings, and its patina speaks of days gone by.

Architectural Details

Rooms decorated in a traditional style often feature wood trim, such as chair rails, wide crown molding, and tall baseboards, which add to the formal appearance of the space. Typically, such details are painted in a crisp white to either contrast with a boldly painted wall or blend with a neutral-color palette in a room. If your home doesn't already have these ornate details, visit a home center to view the selection. Many moldings are lightweight and are easy to install with minimal tools.

CONTEMPORARY

While traditional interiors are all about refined style that conjures images of European palaces—complete with lavish fabrics and ornate gilded frames—contemporary style is sleek and streamlined, paying homage to the innovation and technology of the mid- and latter part of the 20th century. This style is all about clean, straight lines and uncluttered spaces. The two major influences of contemporary design are Scandinavian (which emphasizes natural wood finishes, minimal surface decoration, and flowing sculptured lines) and German Bauhaus (with a nod to machine-made elements, such as furnishings constructed of modular steel).

FURNISHINGS	Modern designs have clean straight lines and sometimes gentle curves. Legs are often exposed and in chunky shapes. If a furnishing is upholstered, the skirt is either flat or may have a box pleat, with few, if any, additional trimmings.
COLORS	White, black, and neutrals (such as beiges and browns) are the basis for a contemporary space; these "noncolors" provide a sense of serenity and a fresh palette for streamlined furnishings and accessories. Sometimes accessories in vivid tones, warm and cool alike, punch up a contemporary room.
FABRICS	Textural appeal is key in a contemporary space; natural fabrics such as wool, cotton, linen, silk, and jute may be used for window treatments and other soft furnishings.
WINDOW TREATMENTS	Simple treatments, such as streamlined shades and blinds and long solid-color panels, are perfect for contemporary spaces.
FLOOR COVERINGS	Sleek surfaces, including vinyl, light-tone wood, and low-pile carpets, work well in contemporary spaces.
LIGHTING	Fixtures made of metal, such as chrome or brushed nickel, that have clean sculptural lines will look at home in a contemporary space.
ACCESSORIES	In keeping with an uncluttered look, decorative accessories and artwork—sculpture, dramatic floral arrangements, brushed-metal accents—should be thoughtfully placed and used sparingly.
OTHER CHARACTERISTICS	Interiors with metal ductwork and exposed brick, such as a loft or former commercial building, easily embrace this style, as do clean, all-white spaces that have the appearance of an art gallery.

Furnishings

Many contemporary-style furnishings incorporate a mix of wood and man-made materials. Whether chairs, sofas, tables, or beds, pieces should lack fancy carved details and other traditional elements.

Authentic contemporary pieces, which include midcentury modern designs by well-known designers like Charles Eames and Mies van der Rohe, are costly, but high-quality reproductions are readily available at a fraction of the price of the "real thing." Because this style embraces pure, uncluttered spaces, putting your money into high-quality pieces—midcentury classics or new designs—that will stand the test of time is a smart investment. If your budget doesn't allow you to splurge on such pieces, look for inexpensive modern furnishings and accessories with sleek lines and a mix of natural and man-made materials produced by mass merchandisers.

With its clean lines and neutral-color upholstery, the chair above left is all about function and contemporary style. The side table with distinct angular lines is a functional piece of art.

The bedroom left exudes contemporary elegance, with its rich color scheme, few well-placed accessories, bursts of color from a floral arrangement, and bold artwork with geometric shapes.

Sculptural handblown glassware is bathed in primary-color light above. Each individual piece is distinct because it has ample "breathing room," but no one item stands out from the rest—contributing to an uncluttered feel.

Colors

Neutral colors, such as white, beige, brown, and black, provide a crisp backdrop for contemporary interiors. But jolts of lively color can energize these restful tones: one focal-point wall in a vivid hue, a brightly colored upholstered furnishing, and artwork or accessories. Punches of color will help the space feel more welcoming than sterile and uninviting.

Fabrics

Because furnishings and accessories in contemporary spaces are often sleek and streamlined, incorporating fabrics can soften the hard edges. To keep the look clean, fabric elements should have minimal embellishment—for instance detail piping and box pleats. Besides being a softening feature, decorative items, like pillows and throws, can introduce punctuations of color and texture without detracting from the overall sharp appearance of the room.

Natural fabrics, such as wool, cotton, linen, leather, and suede, make great companions for a contemporary space. Man-made fabrics like faux fur and suede can also add visual and tactile texture.

To prevent a clean-lined contemporary room from being boring, fabric motifs may be incorporated in the mix. Graphic prints—including abstract forms and motifs that give a nod to the 1950s space race—and geometric patterns work well in modern interiors.

Window Treatments

Leaving a window unadorned—so the strong lines of the window frame are exposed—works well in a contemporary space, although simple treatments that don't detract from the overall look of

The bedroom right is sleek and smooth because of its clean-line furnishings, serene color palette, and minimal but thoughtfully placed decorative items on one wall and on the dressers. Yet it is inviting thanks to a comfortable upholstered chair below right, pillows made of raw silk, tailored bedding, and a crisp fabric canopy.

The combination of a glass base and a textural fabric shade in a dark neutral tone makes the lamp *above left* a handsome fixture for a contemporary space.

Simple glass forms *left* have a sculptural appearance. The single white flower floating in the largest piece makes a quiet artistic statement.

A combination of neutral hues—white walls, dark woods, and rich fabrics in browns and beiges—and natural and man-made materials—wood furnishings, glass lamp bases, a glass-top coffee table, and a metal-frame mirror—make the space *above* a streamlined, sleek room that's perfectly contemporary.

Sensibly Contemporary

For a media room that incorporates contemporary styling, see pages 30–37. The neutral color palette, minimal—yet artistic—accessories, and repetition of geometric shapes all contribute to a clean-line modern space.

ETHNIC

It's no wonder that ethnic decorating has gained in popularity in recent years. Spicy color schemes, natural elements (such as grasses and bamboo) used for flooring and window treatments, and furnishings made of exotic woods all contribute to a clean, relaxed environment that speaks of faraway lands. Rooms decorated with ethnic touches offer a place to restore the soul; exotic elements make each day feel like a vacation in a distant locale. Decorative elements and furnishings with ethnic flair have become widely available at import stores and mass merchandisers, making the style achievable on a budget if authentic, antique pieces are beyond your reach.

FURNISHINGS	Japanese-style furnishings are often simple, unadorned, and made of wood, such as cedar, teak, and maple, that has been stained or varnished. Chinese chests, trunks, cabinets, and more are often lacquered or inlaid with elaborate designs. African-style furnishings are typically made of dark wood and are often carved. Furnishings that look at home in island-style rooms are substantial, visually heavy, and made of mahogany, dark walnut, and teak.
COLORS	Spicy hues, such as reds (a symbol of good luck in China), yellows, and oranges are typical of Asian designs, although serene neutral palettes contribute to a restful Zenlike space. Colors of African-style interiors include neutrals (black, white, and brown) as well as muted reds, yellows, and other earth tones. Neutral tones are also commonplace in tropical style, with bursts of color being introduced through Mother Nature's accessories: plants, fruits, and vegetables.
FABRICS	Hemp, cotton, wool, and silk are perfect companions for exotic Asian spaces. Besides solid-color fabrics (in neutrals and bold warm and cool colors), many patterns and motifs, including florals, geometric shapes, and animals, are popular for Asian styling. Handmade textiles, such as mudcloth, are typical of African-style spaces. Exotic decors also abound in natural fabrics like cotton and mosquito netting.
WINDOW TREATMENTS	Window treatments for Asian, African, and island-style interiors are softly structured: bamboo shades, matchstick blinds, and softly flowing panels made of silk and cotton.
FLOOR COVERINGS	Natural floor coverings, such as bamboo and stone tile, and rugs made of sisal and sea grass are popular in Asian, African, and tropical spaces.
LIGHTING	Rice paper lanterns are typical Asian light fixtures, while lamps with wood bases and simple neutral-color shades are nice companions to African- and island-style interiors.
ACCESSORIES	Asian-style decorative elements include teapots, accessories made of or embellished with ivory and marble, large plants that introduce a natural touch, and folding screens. African-style accessories include carved animal sculptures and masks, pillows made of handmade textiles, and painted pottery. Island-style spaces are filled with accessories made of leather, cane, and ornate inlaid woods.
OTHER CHARACTERISTICS	*Feng shui*—the Asian art of achieving balance of energy and good fortune—has gained popularity in recent years.

The most popular ethnic styles featured on *Sensible Chic* include Asian (both Japanese and Chinese), African, and "island" (incorporating tropical elements from the West Indies and refined Victorian design from British rule). These will be outlined on the following pages. Other popular styles include Moroccan (featuring colorful mosaics, vivid jewel tones, and pillows made of luxurious fabrics), Indian (with bold jewel tones, silk sari fabrics, and gold embellishments), and Native American (featuring handmade blankets and fine beadwork).

Furnishings

Asian-style furnishings typically sit low to the ground and are made of a variety of hardwoods, such as teak and rosewood. Furnishings may be left natural, stained, or covered in layers of black or brightly colored lacquer (which is especially typical of Chinese pieces). Bamboo, rattan, and wicker are also popular materials for furnishings. Japanese furnishings are often simple and streamlined, while Chinese pieces may have elaborate inlays of wood or mother-of-pearl.

African furnishings are often heavy—visually and physically—and are made of medium- and dark-stained hardwoods. These furnishings are often carved with traditional African motifs, such as animals and ancient symbols.

Island-style furnishings are also made of high-quality hardwoods, but stylewise they have a pared-down Victorian elegance. Strong straight lines, dark finishes, and inlays of wood or leather are common.

The tropical-style space above left is filled with elements that contribute to the island feel: dark woods; streamlined furnishings with strong lines; materials such as leather, linen, and silk; luscious fruits and plants; and a large sisal rug.

Pottery in spirited red and neutral tones, highly textured table linens, and ornate chopsticks denote an Asian dining space left.

The trunk above is typical of island style: It features inlaid woods and strong lines and is topped with tropical fruits in a bowl and candles that lend a subtle romantic glow.

The substantial buffet top right has bold carved details; it is a handsome addition to a room with African touches.

From the light-color walls and flooring to the bedding, neutral colors abound in the serene bedroom above right. The natural touches, including tall grasses, and shoji-look panels that serve as closet doors, also usher in quiet elegance.

Colors

Neutral earth tones provide a clean backdrop for Asian, African, and island styles. Warm up these serene palettes with color on walls; accents like pillows; and paintings, prints, and fabrics used as wall-hung art. While Asian decorating styles may incorporate bright reds and cool, crisp blues (think kimono silks), African palettes tend to be more earthy and plant-derived. Island-style interiors get a color boost from natural elements like lush green plants.

Light-filtering rice paper shades, like those left, are a common sight in rooms decorated in ethnic styles.

Fabrics

Natural fabrics, including hemp, silk, cotton, and wool, are popular in all the ethnic decorating styles featured here. In spaces with Asian elements, fabrics dyed with natural colors like indigo and red, silks with elaborate floral embroidery, and printed cottons are popular for throws, pillows, and upholstered furnishings.

African fabrics most often seen in interiors are mudcloth painted in natural hues, soft kasai velvets with mazelike motifs, and wax and fancy prints in bold colors and a wide array of motifs. All these fabrics find uses as pillows and window treatments and for upholstered furnishings.

Island-style interiors typically feature highly textured fabrics left in their natural colors as a nod to the outdoors. These breezy fabrics, which include mosquito netting, are popular for bedding, fabric canopies, and window treatments.

Window Treatments

Window coverings in all ethnic decorating styles share common characteristics: flowing fabrics like soft sheers and blinds and shades made of natural materials such as bamboo. If window treatment hardware, including rods and finials, is visible, it should be simple, clean-lined, and made of metal or wood.

Floor Coverings

Natural elements also abound in floor coverings: While neutral-color carpeting works well in any space decorated in an ethnic style, wood, bamboo, and stone are also commonly used. Rugs help to warm up a floor. In Asian-style rooms rugs made of jute, sisal, and sea grass look right at home. Add a fabric band to the rug for a punch of color on the floor. Oriental rugs can also be used for an Asian-style room with traditional elements (including antique porcelains and furnishings). African decor may also incorporate rugs made of natural materials, but area rugs featuring African motifs and animals are also suitable. Rooms with a tropical atmosphere will benefit from a rug made of natural materials, such as sea grass and sisal, that promote an island feel.

Lighting

Whether it's an overhead fixture, a lamp on a table, or a sconce hung on a wall, lighting for ethnic spaces should consist of materials that complement the other

Sensibly Exotic

For a formal sitting room that is steeped in ethnic elegance—with exotic accessories and a worldly mix of fabrics—see pages 38–45. For a clean and serene bedroom that incorporates Asian touches, including dark-tone furnishings with ethnic appeal, see pages 54–61.

Muted earth tones and the use of ethnic motifs make this rug *right* a nice companion for a room styled with ethnic touches.

elements used throughout the space. In Asian decor, light-color rice paper shades are popular, while a mixture of wood (for the base) and paper or highly textured fabric (for the shade) will accentuate island- or African-style interiors.

Accessories

In all the ethnic decorating styles highlighted here, natural elements like stone, bamboo, wicker, and paper are common. However, each style outlined in this section has its own unique decorative elements.

In Asian decor, blue and white porcelain, bamboo-handle teapots in simple shapes, Chinese wedding baskets made of bamboo, Buddha statues, and bonsai trees are popular. Additional materials commonly seen in rooms decorated in an Asian style include marble, ivory, and mother-of-pearl. Japanese shoji screens or screens that are ornately carved are often seen in Asian-style spaces; they add an element of height that offsets low-lying furnishings and offer a stylish way to hide clutter. On walls handmade paper, pictorial scenes, and Asian calligraphy look just right.

African-style interiors are punctuated with animal prints, wood carvings of animals, ceremonial masks, and elements made of stone, wood, and natural grasses. Drums, dolls, and other functional pieces also work well for additional features.

Island-style spaces often incorporate ornamental carvings, indigenous woods (such as mahogany and teak), and prints featuring natural scenes, like botanicals in simple frames.

An Introduction to *Feng Shui*

Feng shui is an ancient Eastern art that strives to improve health, wealth, and happiness by encouraging—and maximizing—positive energy and harmony in all aspects of our lives. In the home this is achieved by properly placing furniture, accessories, and lighting; selecting harmonizing colors; choosing materials that positively affect the "chi" (life force of animate objects) of the home; and by decluttering.

The space top left abounds with African flair: Tall lamps with animal-print shades flank an ornate mirror made of wood, while decorative accessories made of natural elements (including shells) and a hand-dyed textile add character to the display.

An ornately carved screen in a dark wood is perfect for the Asian-style space above left.

A mix of colors and natural elements is perfect for the African-style dining room above. A twig place mat, a napkin in muted tones, and dishware with stylized animal motifs are set on a heavy wood table for ethnic elegance.

Any room in the home can benefit from cottage-style touches. The young girl's bedroom above abounds in cottage charm: a white painted bed with birdhouse finials; colorful doll clothes hung from the bedposts; a mix of floral, check, and solid-color fabrics on the bed; and whimsical designs painted on the pale yellow walls.

Crackle paint finishes—created in such colors as cherry red, mustard yellow, and deep blue—are commonly seen in country and cottage rooms. Use finishes like this on cabinets, as shown above right, wood furnishings, and even walls.

A pile of pillows in solid colors and a mix of patterns—including various florals and pretty checks—contributes to the comfy, inviting atmosphere in the cottage-style bedroom right. Many of the fabrics are quilted, offering quaint country charm.

through colors (white complemented by blue, pink, green, and yellow) and motifs (including botanicals and seaside themes).

Furnishings

Wood furnishings—typically made of pine and oak—abound in rooms with country and cottage flair. Vintage pine harvest tables, pie safes, blanket chests, and wingback chairs with clean lines and uncomplicated details are throwbacks to a simpler time. Some wood furnishings may have turned legs for subtle flair; hardware is typically solid and chunky.

Wicker is a great companion for country- and cottage-style spaces: It adds a rough natural texture to the mix and can be softened with the addition of cushions, pillows, and throws. If you find wicker pieces with weathered paint finishes, embrace them for their worn appearance.

Upholstered pieces, such as sofas and chairs, typically have simple, clean lines; many are overstuffed for added comfort.

Casual embellishments, including buttons, fringe trim, and even dressmaker details like softly sculpted pleats and piping, contribute to the comfortable feel without being overdone.

When choosing furnishings for your country or cottage space, think comfort, coziness, and time spent with family and friends. As you search, don't limit yourself to typical "indoor" furnishings: Benches and chairs meant for outdoor use can look equally at home in your living room or bedroom. And, for the ultimate in relaxation, incorporate a rocking chair into your retreat!

Colors

In a country-style space classic red, white, and blue, as well as sunny yellows and springy greens, look right at home. Dress a cottage-style space in Mother Nature's palette: pinks and reds, lilac, soft blue, and quiet yellows and greens. In both country and cottage decorating, neutrals, such as white, cream, and an array of brown hues, keep the feeling calm and relaxed; white especially sets a soothing backdrop for any hue you choose for furnishings, fabrics, and accessories.

Fabrics

Natural fabrics, including cotton and wool, suit both the country and cottage decorating style. For a casual cottage space, incorporate floral chintzes, embroidered linens, and crisp stripes and plaids for casual (but never sloppy) slipcovers, cushion covers, window treatments, and pillows. Little details—buttons, soft ruffles, and fringe—make a cottage-style space all the more relaxed and welcoming.

Make It Cottage

To make any furnishing suit a cottage-style space, paint it with a wash of white or casually slipcover it in a striped, floral, or plaid fabric; add a box pleat or a lace edging to enhance the cottage look. As long as the look is loose and casual, it doesn't matter what lies beneath.

Keep It Clean

With the wide array of colors and patterns—and the range of decorative accessories—that work in country- and cottage-style spaces, the look could easily become cluttered and unorganized. To ensure a serene, quiet space, follow these tips for displaying accessories with ease:

- Vary the height of items for visual interest on a tabletop display or in a bookcase. To give short items a boost, stack them on vintage books or weathered pedestals.

- Mix up the texture: Pairing a smooth, curvy white pitcher and a textured element such as a basket or hat is casually chic.

- Keep the look light by using asymmetrical groupings of items; symmetrically balanced pairs of items can look too formal and contrived.

- Group like items together, such as a collection of silver teapots or vintage clocks, to give them a sense of importance rather than sprinkling them throughout a space. Similarly, display a family of items, such as birdhouses, watering cans, and garden tools, together to reinforce a theme.

When searching for wood furnishings, look for medium- and dark-tone pieces made of oak and walnut that have an elegant look and feel. Details such as X-shape stretchers on tables and chairs and chrome or silver pulls and knobs on dressers and cabinets complement the chic look.

Alternately, search for furnishings made of sleek chrome, steel, aluminum, and glass or mirrors for an edgier look. Upholstered or wood furnishings that incorporate details of man-made materials also fit the chic style.

Colors

For a chic space use a mix of neutral and bold hues, with one being dominant and the other playing a supporting role. For instance, white or light-color walls will allow furnishings and accessories in vibrant hues like lime green, fuchsia, and orange to be the focus of the space, while a sense of intimacy can be achieved in a chic space by splashing an eye-popping color on the walls and using neutral-tone furnishings for balance.

Fabrics

Dress a chic space in luxurious fabrics that make the space look and feel rich. Use satin, silk (the epitome of glamour when used on a bed!), velvet, and chenille. If you desire pattern, look for subtle tone-on-tone fabrics in geometric prints, including diamonds, checks, zigzags, and chevrons. For a trendy look, incorporate batiks and animal prints with graphic appeal like zebra stripes. Use them on the floor and on decorative accents like pillows.

Window Treatments

Streamlined window treatments—with no frills or only minimal embellishment—work well in chic interiors. Use heavy fabrics like velvet for rich window coverings in a more formal space, such as a dining room. Hang window treatments from clean-lined rods made of metal or wood painted to complement the decor of the room. Alternately, high-quality wood or metal blinds can look sleek and sophisticated in a chic-style space.

Floor Coverings

As with many decorating styles, hardwood floors offer a rich base on which to build a chic look. To warm a wood floor and to add comfort underfoot—not to mention introduce doses of color and pattern to

The bedroom right is the perfect mix of streamlined design and casual elegance—all the while being undeniably chic. The bold cherry red walls, playful bedding with embroidered butterflies, and natural touches such as tall grasses and a textural sisal rug offer pleasing contrast to the dark furnishings.

a room—bring in plush rugs in animal prints or strong geometric shapes. For a fun, trendy look, seek out faux fur rugs or rugs with a shaggy pile. As an alternate to wood floors, choose carpeting in a neutral hue.

Lighting

From oversize crystal chandeliers to table lamps made of glass or metal and topped with a shade of silk, chic spaces revel in all things that speak of the good life. For a room that's high on the glamour scale, select fixtures that are lavished in detail, such as crystal drops; for a more streamlined look, choose contemporary-style fixtures made of metal or glass.

Accessories

An exciting array of accessories can accentuate a chic space. The look can be over-the-top with faux fur throws, brightly colored pottery, and artwork with contemporary subject matter like abstract geometric shapes. For a more streamlined setting, choose elegant glassware, silver serving pieces, and black and white artwork that exudes Hollywood glamour. Regardless of which side you navigate toward, keep the look clean and sleek. Incorporate bevel-edge mirrors and brightly polished silver furniture hardware, and feel free to mix in exotic influences, such as lacquered screens, animal prints, and stylized flowers and fauna motifs.

Chic style is all about refined elegance. In the space above, an elegant glass chandelier and a painting—in bright fashion colors—promote the chic feel.

Part Hollywood glamour, part sleek and contemporary, chic style is highlighted in the dining space above. The curvy metal vase with a casual arrangement of tulips and silver-rim dishware set on a dark-stained table have an elegant feel.

A print of a man in a tuxedo right is chic in its subject matter, its black and white scheme, and the triple mat and clean-lined black frame.

The Ultimate Sensible Shopping Guide

You've had an opportunity to leisurely stroll through ten outstanding rooms featured on *Sensible Chic* that are inspired by expensive designer spaces—and to discover ways to achieve a pricey look for less. You've also learned about the various attributes of five popular decorating styles—traditional, contemporary, ethnic, country, and chic—and you've identified what style best matches your personality. Along the way you've undoubtedly begun to envision how you can transform each and every room of your home to achieve a high-end look for less. The next step? It's time to put your decorating dreams into motion by filling your home with the furnishings and accessories that suit both your style and your budget.

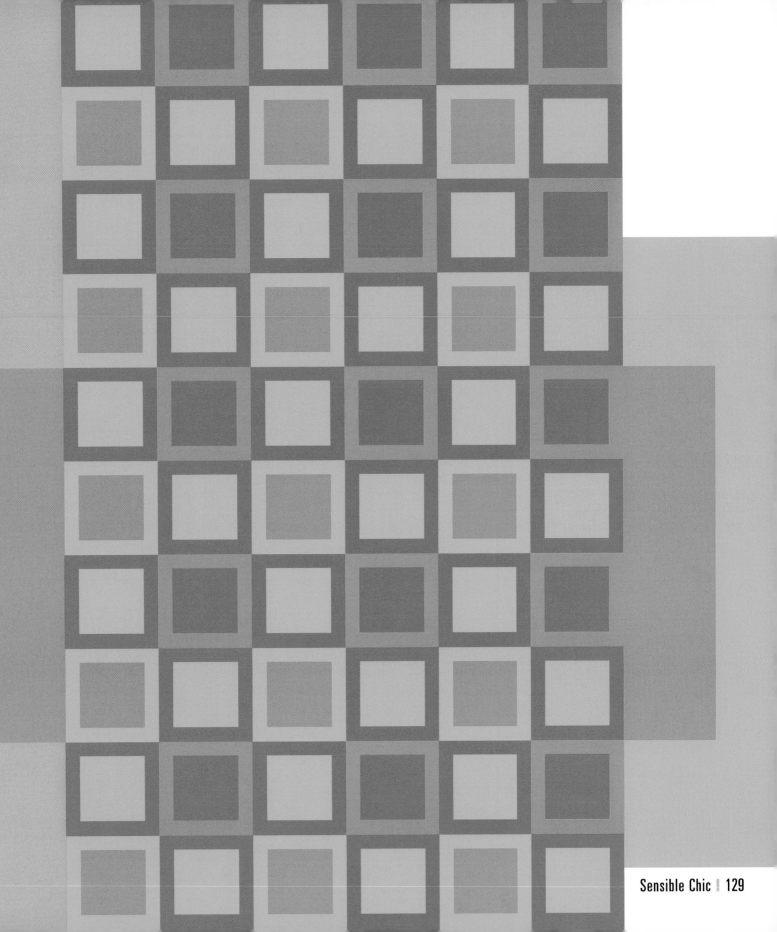

Name-Your-Price Decorating

The goal of this section is to take you through the process of designing the room of your dreams—regardless of the type of room or the specific style—by outlining a process of tried-and-true techniques used by professional designers. Once you have mastered the strategies covered on the following pages—from determining what you need in your new Sensibly Chic space to budgeting and determining the best places to shop to get just what you want—you will be well on your way to creating spaces that are tailored to the way you live at a price you can afford. Throughout this journey you will discover how furnishings and accessories differ at various prices and how these differences affect your purchasing decisions and fit your lifestyle.

Make Room for Mad Money

You've budgeted carefully and planned to buy your furnishings in the order of their functional importance, and then you see it: The painting you just can't live without. The vase that would look just perfect on the mantel. A throw pillow covered in vintage silk. You see it, you love it—and you know you'd have to be crazy to pass it up. That's why you'll want to include some mad money in your budget: a few—or a few hundred—dollars that you can pull out of a pocket when your sensible shopping turns up a once-in-a-lifetime find.

Plan for Success Before you start shopping, make a list of everything you think you might need—or want—in your new Sensibly Chic room. List everything, from the largest, most functional pieces (a sofa or mattress) to the smallest decorative details (finials for a lamp or a curtain rod). Next, review the list and eliminate any items you already own that you can reuse in your newly decorated space, such as an old chair that could be made as good as new with a little elbow grease and some fresh paint. What remains will serve as your shopping list. If you plan to replace existing furniture, you'll have a bit more leeway in terms of what to buy first and what can wait. But, it is still important to have an overall shopping list so you can determine a reasonable budget before you hit the stores.

Now, rank the items in order of importance. See what you'll need to buy first and what can wait until later. If you're starting with an empty room, you'll want to begin with whatever it takes to make the room functional, for example a couch or other seating for a living room, or a bed and someplace to store clothes for a bedroom. Next, plan to purchase the things that will expand the room's utility. In a bedroom that might be a reading chair, while in a living room it might be an ottoman that can also serve as a coffee table. Then, when you have most of your furniture, you can dedicate time and energy—and your budget—to selecting accessories, like throw pillows and artwork, that really pull a room together. The bedroom *right* is a great example of this design process.

Budget Basics There are two good ways to determine a decorating budget. The first is to look at how much money you have available (money you've been saving every month for just this purpose, or perhaps your income tax refund), and then shop for the pieces that fit into that budget—just as *Sensible Chic*'s Sensible Shoppers do week after week. For example, if you have a fixed sum of $3,000 to spend on a living room, you will likely shop for a sofa and chairs, occasional tables, lighting, and accessories. But the trick is determining the combination of items and prices that will allow you to get everything you need

▶ **Sensible Shopper's Tip** *Sensible Chic* Design Coordinator Jen Jordan suggests that before you go shopping you should ask yourself what you can make for your new room. Can you build a coffee table yourself? Sew curtains? Doing it yourself will help you save money—and get exactly the look you want.

Step One Using what you have on hand may not be overly fashionable, but you need to start somewhere! Although this bedroom is filled with hand-me-downs—an old dresser with dark stain, a chair that's better suited for outdoor use, and a cardboard box that stands in as a bedside table—the homeowner invested in clean white bedding and a comfortable mattress. Together, the bedding and mattress offer a great starting point for something more stylish down the road.

Step Two With a splash of color on the walls (a light aqua blue), a stylish new dresser and bedside table, a platform bed frame, decorative glassware, and inexpensive white paper lanterns, this room is becoming a space that's both functional and fun to be in. To firmly establish the bed as the focal point in this room, a frame of 1x4s capped with crown molding serves as a mock headboard. To further emphasize this treatment, the area within the frame is painted a deeper aqua color than the surrounding walls.

Step Three With a palette of white and aqua firmly established, this bedroom is now kicked into color overdrive with the addition of a colorful graphic quilt above the bed, a sleek chair covered in lush purple upholstery, comfy purple and aqua bedding, bright aqua storage boxes, and oversize rugs in purple and aqua. The rugs not only warm the wood floor but also repeat the circle motifs used throughout the space.

Avoid the Credit Card Crunch

It may be tempting to buy furniture on credit before you have accumulated the money to pay for it, but keep your plastic in your pocket. Buying expensive pieces on credit can cost you dearly in the long run. A sofa on sale for 20 percent off may sound like a big bargain, but if it takes you two years to pay off the bill, the interest and finance charges will actually make your sofa more expensive than if you had bought it for cash at full price!

Before you invest in new furnishings, determine if you can perk up an existing piece with a coat of paint and new hardware, as shown below.

without exceeding your spending limit.

At first you may be disappointed to realize that you can't purchase the $2,000 sofa you love and a $1,000 chair (at least not if you also want to buy a lamp) on your fixed $3,000 budget. But, there is always more than one way to achieve the look you're after.

If you're having trouble finding an affordable version of an item on your wish list, think about what drew you to your inspiration piece, then look for pieces that have some of those same design elements. For example, if you can't afford an antique Chinese wedding cabinet, you may choose to buy a bamboo media cabinet from an import store instead. The look isn't identical, but the Sensibly Chic piece will give you the storage you need with the Asian flair that made the inspiration piece so attractive. Or say you like the look of a bright pink cashmere throw—but not the $400 price tag. For a similar dose of softness and bright color,

you can purchase a fuchsia chenille coverlet for just a fraction of the price. This kind of creative substitution will help you stay within your fixed budget while achieving the look that reflects your personality.

If the fixed-sum approach to budgeting feels too restrictive, try the second method of determining your buying power: Shop around for a while and then add up the cost of the pieces you think you'd like to purchase. Figure out how many months or years it will take you to accumulate the money to pay for the items on your list. For example, if you decide that you'd like to purchase a sofa that costs $2,500, you may not be able to afford to buy it today, but you can start saving toward that purchase immediately. Can you save $100 a week? You'll be able to buy the sofa in about six months. Can't cut $100 a week out of your current expenses? How about saving half that much—and buying the sofa a year from now? (Skip that gourmet coffee on your way to work every morning and you'll save about $90 a month.)

Twelve months may sound like a long time to wait when you've found the perfect piece of furniture, but you can use that time to your best advantage. In that period you can browse for subsequent purchases, learn which stores hold sales at what times of the year, and tackle the repairs and do-it-yourself projects that will help create a clean, fresh backdrop for your prized piece.

Remember: Good design takes time. On television a room can go from empty to embellished in half an hour, but in real life

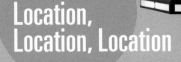

$178   **$463**   **$603**

Location, Location, Location

Before you decide how much to spend on an item, consider where it will be placed and how prominently it will be seen. An overhead light fixture that hangs high on a hallway ceiling may only get a passing glance. It may be wise to select a less expensive fixture that doesn't need to stand up to scrutiny—and dedicate what you saved to a fixture that will hang above your dining room table and be at the center of conversation.

These three schoolhouse-style light fixtures may share like materials, a similar shape, and nearly the exact color of glass, but they differ significantly in price. When shopping for fixtures—or any furnishing or accessory—consider how and where the piece will be used to determine what level of quality you need.

it takes most home decorators—even professional designers—months, or even years, to find the perfect furnishings and accessories for a room. So don't try to race through your decorating project. Take time and enjoy the process of pulling together pieces to create your dream space. Consider various options and avoid the temptation to buy something just because the price is super-low. Ultimately you will have a room you really love and can enjoy for years.

When Is a Bargain Really a Bargain? Once you have decided what pieces you want to buy, you'll certainly want to acquire them at the best possible price. But low price alone does not always equal a great bargain. A trendy $100 armchair that breaks the first time you sit on it is certainly not a great

deal, while a timelessly elegant chair that costs $1,000 but turns a room from drab to dramatic and lasts for three generations can be the buy of a lifetime. Similarly, a rug with a rock-bottom price may seem like a bargain, but if it's going to look worn and dirty five minutes after you place it in your entranceway, you are not really getting a great value. Pay a bit more for a rug that will stand up to everyone who treads on it for years to come, and you've scored a super deal.

So, how can you tell whether you're spending your money wisely? Is there really any difference between a $500 chain store sofa and a piece that costs $2,500? And, why do some lamps cost $750, while others can be yours for just a tenth of the price? The comparisons on the following pages will help you get

an idea of how much you should expect to pay for different levels of quality—and how to get the most for your decorating dollar. The key principle to remember is that by surveying items at varying price and quality levels, you will be able to prioritize and select the right pieces for your lifestyle. For instance, if your living room doubles as a playroom, spending $1,000 on a lamp that may get knocked off a table probably isn't a wise choice; however, if you place that same lamp in a no-kids-allowed formal dining space or master suite, the lamp will likely last a lifetime. This also allows you to pick and choose what's important to you: You may decide to splurge on a luxury item such as fine, high-thread-count bed linens, but opt for a low-cost area rug for a room that doesn't receive much foot traffic.

So-fa So Good!

A sofa is usually the most expensive piece of furniture in a living room, with prices ranging from a few hundred dollars to several thousand. To decide how much of your budget to allocate to this central piece, consider how you are going to use it: Is your living room an adults-only space, where you entertain to impress important business associates? Go for the best sofa—perhaps covered in a luxurious fabric—you can possibly afford. Is the piece going to serve as Super Bowl Party Central or your kids' indoor trampoline? Pick a less expensive piece with a durable fabric like denim or twill or a piece you can easily slipcover.

Construction Techniques

What's the difference between a dovetail joint and a butt joint? A dovetail joint is made of fingerlike projections (or angled wedges) that interlock. Secured with glue, dovetail joints offer maximum support and strength. Butt joints are of a much simpler—and not as sturdy—construction: Two pieces of wood are set against one another and glued or nailed together.

Some sofas come with their own slipcovers. These pieces fit the frame exactly, but they are removable for washing and then easily go back on the sofa. You can also buy slipcovers from a home products store or catalog, usually for much less than you'd pay for slipcovers available from the sofa manufacturer. While mail-order and chain store slipcovers are a good choice for standard-size sofas, they can look sloppy or ill-fitting on sofas with an unusual shape or size. If your sofa has unique dimensions, consider having custom slipcovers made at a local workroom (or make them yourself if you are a skilled stitcher). Custom slipcovers can be expensive, but they will keep your investment looking clean and neat.

Before purchasing a sofa, sit on it for a while—and lie down too if you're a sofa snoozer. Pick up any detachable cushions and turn them over to make sure the fabric on the underside looks as good as what's on top. Being able to flip and rotate the cushions will help your sofa look good longer.

Use this section to educate yourself on the differences between a budget sofa and a much more expensive piece, and then decide which features you're willing to compromise on and which are absolute "musts."

Although these sofas may look similar— their shapes, the color of their upholstery, and their size—they range greatly in price.

▶ **Sensible Shopper's Tip** Before you fork over big bucks for a piece of furniture because it's "built to last forever," ask yourself if you're really going to want it forever. The average moderately priced sofa will last 15 years, which is probably longer than you will love it anyway. Unless you are buying a piece so simple and timeless that it can be reinvented with pillows, throws, and slipcovers every time your tastes change, consider buying something less expensive. Otherwise, you may feel chained to that chair or sofa for years.

$800

SPRINGS The springs in a budget sofa are S-shape and may sag or give out over time. Springs in mid-range sofas are tied eight ways or made of higher-quality S coils to help the sofa maintain its shape and spring. The most costly sofas almost exclusively have eight-way hand-tied springs.

UPHOLSTERY Budget sofas are usually available in a limited color palette—often with lower-quality fabric options—and patterns will seldom match. Choices in color and fabric widen with mid-price pieces: Some sofas offer the option of "customer's own material," or COM, in which you provide the fabric of your choice that's upholstered onto the frame at the factory. High-end sofas offer nearly unlimited choices. All work is custom-done, so you can choose almost any fabric imaginable.

LEGS In a lower-price sofa, legs may be made of metal or plastic and are screwed into the main frame. Legs on a moderately priced sofa may be a part of the overall frame, or they may be attached at the end of construction. In high-price sofas, the wood legs are a part of the frame, offering extra stability, while support legs prevent a high-end sofa from sagging.

FRAME Budget sofa frames are made of plywood and particleboard, with joints that are butted or glued together. Most joints in a mid-price sofa are joined by dowels or dovetails; some pieces may be butted or nailed in place. The frame is often made of kiln-dried hardwood. Extremely sturdy dowel or dovetail-joint construction distinguishes the fine construction of high-end sofas. The frames are made of kiln-dried hardwood.

SEATS AND CUSHIONS In a low-cost sofa, cushions and pillows are usually stuffed with a block of foam that may lose its shape over time. Moderately priced sofas often have a core of foam that is surrounded by fluffier polyfill for increased comfort. Cushions in the most expensive sofas are made of either a foam/down combination (that readily springs into shape) or are 100 percent down (a luxurious option that requires "pillow plumping").

$4,400

$1,800

Case in Point: Dressers, Bureaus, Bookcases

Don't let insider lingo intimidate you. When furniture salespeople refer to "case goods," they're simply talking about bookcases, dressers, and other non-upholstered pieces, usually made of wood or wood look-alikes. As with all other home furnishings, price and value can vary widely, and both your budget and needs will dictate your decision on how much to spend.

FURNITURE MATERIALS
Woods to Know

Having a basic understanding of the materials used to construct furniture will help you make an educated buying decision.

WOODS: Hardwoods—cherry, maple, mahogany, oak, walnut, birch, ebony, poplar, rosewood, and teak—are more durable and typically more expensive than softwoods. Softwoods—yellow pine, white pine, and cedar—are more widely available but are susceptible to marring and denting.

COMPOSITES: These are manufactured wood products, such as plywood and particleboard. Plywood is comprised of multiple layers of thin sheets of wood that are glued and pressed together. It is strong and resistant to warping, shrinking, and swelling. Particleboard is made of sawdust, small wood chips, and glue or resin—which may include formaldehyde—that have been mixed together and pressure-treated. Particleboard splits easily.

VENEERS: Veneer is a thin sliver of wood applied to a wood or plywood base. When shopping for furnishings with veneers, ensure the veneer is tightly attached to the base material; if there are gaps it may pop loose.

Do you always cover your dining table with a tablecloth? If so you can get away with a slightly lower-quality piece than if you always leave the table exposed. Just be sure any dining table you purchase is strong enough so it won't shake when an etiquette-challenged guest tries to cut his or her steak with a butter knife. Dining chairs have to be sturdy too: You and your guests will slide them toward and away from the table thousands of times over the years. Before you buy a chair, sit in it for a while to make sure it's comfortable, and check the joints to make sure they are smooth, solid, and ready to take on even your least-careful guest.

Bedroom furniture also varies widely in price and construction—and different pieces are suitable for different needs. Will your dresser be covered with photos and knickknacks? If so, don't dedicate your money to an extravagantly priced piece with a fancy parquetry top. Are you looking for a piece for a guest room? Good looks may be more important to you than the smoothness of drawer glides, because your piece needs to make a strong first impression but won't actually get much heavy use (unless you use it for storage when guests aren't in town).

The following information will tell you what you can expect to find in dressers at three different retail price points. The two dressers featured—one from a national retailer, the other handmade and hand-painted—have like qualities, but they are priced quite differently.

▶ **Sensible Shopper's Tip** "When you're looking for pieces to help you re-create an inspiration room," says *Sensible Chic* Design Coordinator Jen Jordan, "look at shape before you look at color." For example, if you want a red triangular table, look for a three-sided piece in any color; then paint it the hue you want. This strategy is much easier than trying to turn a red square into a triangle.

MATERIALS Low-cost dressers are usually constructed of particleboard or medium-density fiberboard (MDF) covered with inexpensive wood veneer or a photograph of wood printed on heavy paper. If the inexpensive veneer is scratched or nicked, it is almost impossible to repair. Mid-price dressers are made with a combination of top-quality hardwood and veneers. Scratches in hardwood at this quality level can be buffed out. The most costly of dressers is usually solid hardwood, but high-quality veneers may be used for inlaid designs and other embellishments. Note that the wood in an expensive antique dresser may dry out, making it more likely to crack if positioned too close to a radiator.

USAGE Inexpensive dressers are a good choice for off-season storage or for use as a nightstand by covering the dresser with an interesting fabric. A mid-price dresser is the perfect choice in a small bedroom with space for just a few pieces. Buy something attractive and make every piece count. A high-price dresser is such a star that it seems almost a shame to hide it in a room where you'll spend most of your time with your eyes closed.

STYLING Often, low-price pieces have basic, undistinguished styling, but you can enhance these pieces by repainting or by changing hardware. Dressers in the mid-range are handsome and substantial; upgrading the hardware may enhance the elegant look. The most expensive pieces may be custom-made or hand-embellished, an exclusive designer piece, or an antique; these dressers have distinct styling.

$1,299

JOINTS Joints in a low-cost dresser are glued or butted together. In a moderately priced piece dowels or dovetails may join the joints for extra stability. The highest-quality dressers have dovetail construction throughout. Top-quality carpentry ensures that drawers glide in and out easily.

$5,800

DRAWERS Drawers in inexpensive dressers are made of particleboard or plastic with cardboard bottoms; these drawers may stick when opened. Mid-price dressers have interior drawers made of less expensive wood than the wood on the outside surfaces. Often, wood or metal drawer glides may help drawers slide in and out more smoothly than on a budget dresser. High-end dressers are constructed of top-quality hardwood throughout.

Always Underfoot

If your home has beautiful hardwood or ceramic floors or lush carpeting, you may wish to leave the floor uncovered. But most rooms, even ones that do have lovely floors, look more pulled together with some kind of rug, especially when it brings together all the colors in a room.

Sizing It Up

Whatever type of rug you decide fits your style and your budget, never skimp on size. Placing a 5x8-foot rug in a room that really needs a 9x12-foot rug can make the whole space look out of balance. Not sure how big you need to go? Cut and piece brown kraft paper together in several different sizes—or just use newspapers—and lay them on the floor to see which works best. This will help you determine whether the size you're planning to purchase looks sumptuous or skimpy before you buy.

When you prepare to purchase a rug, ask yourself the following: Are you going to splurge on an antique Chinese silk rug or save on an acrylic piece made in Taiwan last Tuesday? Do you want the plush feel of wool under your bare feet, or would you like to create a more casual look with sisal or sea-grass matting? Do you want to go wall-to-wall with broadloom or maybe off-the-wall with an unusual painted floorcloth?

When shopping for a rug, ask the salesperson to place the rug on the floor so that you can walk on it—shoed and barefoot, if you walk around your home without shoes. How does it feel underfoot?

Get help holding the rug up to light to make sure there are no "bald spots" (places where there is too little pile or where the rug is worn).

Before you restrict yourself to a traditional rug, consider some unique options: Look at industrial carpets or bamboo mats (available at many import stores), and think about painting an unattractive wood floor a bright color or stenciling it.

Of course, there are times when only a classic rug will do. If you're shopping for one, here's what you can expect to get for different prices. *Note: The prices given are for a 5x8-foot rug.*

$278

$1,025

$425

MATERIALS The least expensive rugs are often made of olefin or another synthetic fabric. Mid-price rugs are most often made of wool. Very expensive rugs are made of fine wool and sometimes silk.

PILE The pile in low-cost rugs is often loose, making the pattern appear diffuse. The pile is tight in a moderately priced rug; these rugs feel full and luxurious underfoot. In the most expensive pieces, the pile is very tight; the rug feels velvety and fine.

DURABILITY The price and durability of low-cost rugs are good bets for a high-traffic area. They also work well in crowded rooms that appear unbalanced without a rug—but in which only a very small portion of the carpet will actually show. Rugs that are moderately priced work anywhere and can stand up to several years' worth of everyday wear and tear. The most expensive rugs are durable and repel spills, but if you purchase a handwoven antique, it may be fragile and not suited for high-traffic areas or rooms in which food and beverages are served.

COLOR The colors of an inexpensive rug may be overly bright and artificial-looking or they may be muddy and dull. Typically, the colors of a mid-price rug look clean and new, but they are not overly bright or artificial-looking. Many of the most expensive rugs are precious antiques from across the globe. With age the colors in these extraordinary pieces may have faded.

Beddie Buys

Is your bedroom a romantic haven for just you and your mate, or is it a second family room? Do you use your bed just for sleeping, or is it also your home office, laundry-sorting station, and baby's changing pad? A realistic assessment of your needs and lifestyle will help you decide whether to splurge or save on your sheets and duvet covers.

If it's pampering and romance you're after, go for the most luxurious bedding you can afford. But if your bed is going to do double-duty as a gym, you'll want less-expensive bedding that you can replace without breaking the bank.

What determines the difference in the price of bedding? The biggest factor is thread count (the number of threads per inch of fabric). The higher the thread count, the finer—and softer—the individual threads, and the softer and more luxurious the sheets. Natural fibers, usually cotton and sometimes silk, will cost more than a cotton/polyester blend, but they also require more care and attention because they wrinkle easily.

To decide what your bedding budget should be, use the following information to help you determine what you can expect to get for your money. The prices provided *opposite* are based on queen-size flat sheets.

Quilts: What to Use, What to Admire

Not all bedding is made for beds. Antique quilts can cost thousands of dollars and are often very fragile. Similarly, many quilts, such as the example *below left*, are high-price designer originals intended as artwork. To preserve antique or one-of-a-kind quilts, keep them off your bed, and display them out of direct sunlight to prevent fading. If the quilt is especially fragile, consider having it professionally framed. If you want the look of a vintage or custom-designed quilt on your bed, a mass-produced quilt like the example *below right* is a better bet: It's machine-washable, it's replaceable, and it is very reasonably priced in comparison.

$1,000

$185

CARE Low-cost sheets are usually permanent press. It is recommended to remove mid-price sheets from the dryer and fold immediately to reduce wrinkles; iron pillowcases and the part of the sheet that turns over your duvet or comforter. Expensive bedding deserves care: Sheets this luxurious should be ironed.

USAGE The lowest-price sheets are great for kids' rooms: The price is so low you won't mind replacing the stegosaurus sheets when that dinosaur fad gives way to an airplane obsession. Mid-price sheets are comfortable enough to make sleep-time sensuous. Sheets in this price range are a good choice if you want to allocate a large part of your budget to a duvet cover and throw pillows. High-price sheets are worth the splurge if you sleep in the buff or live in a warm climate where sheets will not be covered by a heavy blanket or duvet. Sheets of this quality are also a great treat for your guest room.

HEMS AND STITCHES The hems and stitches of low-price sheets may be crooked. With increased quality comes increased price: Moderately priced sheets have small, even stitches. High-end sheets have stitches so perfect they are nearly invisible.

THREAD COUNT Most inexpensive sheets have a thread count around 200. Sheets that are moderately priced often have 250–300 threads per inch. High-end sheets usually have a thread count of 400 or more.

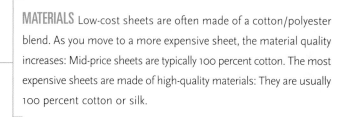

$180

MATERIALS Low-cost sheets are often made of a cotton/polyester blend. As you move to a more expensive sheet, the material quality increases: Mid-price sheets are typically 100 percent cotton. The most expensive sheets are made of high-quality materials: They are usually 100 percent cotton or silk.

$55

COLOR AND PATTERN The least expensive sheets are often available in a wide array of colors and patterns, including large splashy prints and child-theme patterns. More expensive sheets are also available in a wide range of colors and prints, although the patterns may be more refined. The most expensive sheets and comforters generally come in just a few colors and very subtle patterns.

$20

You Do Windows

In public areas of your home, such as the living room and dining room, curtains may not be an immediate necessity. In the bedroom, however, you'll want to cover your windows for privacy. Either way, when you do start shopping for window treatments, the array of choices and qualities is almost endless.

Ready-made curtain panels come in hundreds of colors and patterns. Want a solid burgundy velvet drape? You'll find one at almost any good-size discount store. Looking for sheers made out of Indian sari fabrics? Flip through the pages of a catalog or browse through your local import store, and you're likely to find a dozen or two. From stripes to solids and florals to foulards, ready-made drapes can help a room look finished and elegant—and they're generally inexpensive.

While such ready-made treatments are relatively low cost and the selection is great, they're not right for every window. In a room where a window is a focal point, you may want to spend a bit more on ready-made curtains that are lined for body and drama or on custom-made drapes in an unusual fabric or style. If your window is an odd shape, or if you want a unique valance or cornice, you may need to have treatments custom made. No matter which way you go, you can save money if you know what to look for and how much each of the different options should cost.

Regardless of whether you purchase ready-mades or splurge for custom treatments, carefully consider the rods and other hardware, such as finials and curtain clips. These decorative details can accentuate even the most ordinary of panels and continue a decorating theme. Materials for these all-important elements range from wood to various sheens and textures of metal; finials can be simple balls or more elaborate faux jewel-encrusted baubles.

Measure Twice, Buy Once

Be sure you have measured your windows accurately before buying nonreturnable window treatments. Just as too-short pants can make an otherwise chic outfit look sloppy, too-short curtains can ruin the whole look of a room. If you are paying to have expensive window treatments custom-made, insist that the workroom send someone to your home to measure; that way any errors in the size of the finished product will be their fault—and they will be liable to replace them.

▶ **Try Before You Buy** Hold the drapes up to a strong light; this is how they will appear when hung in a sunny window. Also check that the hems are straight and the seams aren't puckered—and that the treatments fit over the curtain rods you want.

SIZE Many low-price window treatments are available in one length (or very few choices); if a panel is too long, you may hem it, and if it's too short for your needs, you can stitch on a border in a coordinating fabric or a dressy trim. Ready-made window treatments that are moderately priced are usually available in two or three lengths; hem or add fabric to make one fit your window height properly. If you don't sew, having off-the-rack curtains professionally hemmed or narrowed will still be cheaper than having a custom drapery made. By spending more on custom window treatments you can get the size you need: A professional will measure your window, and the treatment will be exactly the right length.

FABRIC Low-cost window treatments are typically made of synthetic fabrics or inexpensive cotton. More expensive ready-mades are available in a wider variety of fabrics, including light, loose-weave silks. Expensive custom curtains offer unlimited fabric choices. Most often a workroom will make up the drapes in any fabric you choose.

DRESS IT UP Low-price curtains are most often untrimmed, but you may easily embellish them with fringe, beads, or tassels. Some mid-price curtains will already have contrasting piping or trim. Curtains that are high-price will be trimmed to your wishes; however, note that trims may add significantly to the price.

$370

LINING Usually inexpensive curtains are not lined. Curtains in the mid-price range are often—but not always—lined. If you need drapes to block sunlight, look for lined draperies. Lining and interlining give high-end window treatments plenty of body, similar to the skirt of a ball gown.

$129

STITCH QUALITY Because low-cost curtains are machine-hemmed, the stitches may be visible. Expect invisible hemstitches on moderately priced window treatments. Stitches on high-cost curtains should not be visible. To ensure quality workmanship, ask to see samples of a company's work before ordering your curtains.

See the Light

No matter how beautiful your furniture is, no one will be able to enjoy it if the room is pitch-dark. Because of its importance, lighting is one of the very first purchases you will need to make—and it can make a big difference in the finished room.

When shopping for lamps, make sure the piece you choose is approved by the Underwriters Laboratories, which checks electrical products for safety. Secondhand pieces may need to be rewired; if you're not certain about the safety of a flea market lamp, buy a lamp kit at the hardware store and rewire it. For just a few dollars and a couple hours of your time, you can be assured that your flea market find is as safe as it is stylish. (See page 176 for a lamp project that will teach you the basics of lamp wiring; you can use this information to rewire an existing lamp or to make your very own lamp from a teapot, vase, or a stack of books.)

Of course, even safe, well-wired lamps vary in quality. Some are undistinguished, or even sloppily made, while others are works of fine art with hand-painted ceramic bases adorned by the finest silk shades. The following will tell you what you can expect from lamps at different price points.

Can You Spy the Knockoff?

These two lamps may look nearly the same, but they're not: One is manufactured by a well-known pottery company and retails for $395; the other is a chain store knockoff that can be yours for $40. Can you spot the designer original and the less expensive version?

A. Jonathan Adler $395 B. Target $37

A

B

▶ Try Before You Buy Before you purchase a lamp, plug it in and turn it on. Make sure the shape doesn't cast any strange shadows on a wall—and if you're planning to replace the shade, make sure it is a standard size and can be easily changed.

USE Low-cost lamps are a good choice if they will be placed on a side table with many distinctive accessories that will block part of the base and add interest to the tableau. To make an inexpensive lamp look more luxurious, replace its plain lampshade with something more distinct. Lamps that are moderately priced can hold their own on a table, but you'll probably want to add an unusual accessory or two to make the grouping look more personal. To make a simple lamp look more elegant, add braided trim or velvet ribbon at the upper and lower edges of the shade. And, if you opt for an expensive lamp, place it on an uncluttered table where it will be a true focal point.

SHADE Low-cost lampshades are often made of inexpensive paper or synthetic fabric. Shades for mid-price lamps are typically in a basic hue, made of heavy paper or a neutral-color fabric. The most expensive lamps usually have a shade made of pure silk that may be embellished with expensive cording, ribbon, or other trim.

$225

$35

BASE The bases of low-price lamps are made of inexpensive ceramic, metal, or wood. Often, the base is unbalanced and has improper proportions. Moderately priced bases are often made of a higher-quality ceramic, brass, or wrought iron. The base of a high-end lamp may be a one-of-a kind piece of art, such as Italian ceramic or Chinese porcelain. The overall shape and proportion of the base will be balanced and elegant.

CORD The electric cord of an inexpensive lamp may look like plastic and may clash with the lamp base. In a mid-price lamp, the electric cord is better coordinated with the color and style of the lamp base. When you spend a lot you get refinement: The cord of a high-end lamp may be covered in silk.

Where the Buys Are

Once you know what kinds of products you're looking for, the challenge is knowing where to purchase them at the very best price. In this section you'll discover all the best bargain-hunting tricks *Sensible Chic*'s Sensible Shoppers use—they're very happy to spill their secrets! Here's how you can get the most bang for your buck.

The Chain Gang

At first glance, the pieces in national chain stores may look uninspired—and uninspiring. But when you mix them with more exotic pieces or tinker with them just a bit to add some flair, you've got the basis for a chic look at very sensible prices. When you see basics, such as case goods, lampshades and bases, or photo frames in a chain store, ask yourself, "What can I do to this? Can I paint it? Change the knobs? Can I add unusual trim?" With little time or effort you may be able to dress up a bland piece without spending a fortune.

See page 187 for some of the very best chain stores that offer the widest selection of home furnishings and accessories. Their websites will help you find the closest store, and many of the companies sell their products directly over the Internet as well. Not on the web yet? Phone the stores to ask if they have an outpost close to your home.

The Super Sale

It's a designer brand-name item, at a reputable department store—and it's marked down by 50 percent! Most department stores and boutiques run sales, annually or every season, to make room for new merchandise. And while your end-of-season choices may be limited to less popular items (after all, that's why they're still available), you might just fall in love with a "reduced for clearance" item—and love its price too.

The Price of Frame

Chain stores and Internet outlets are often a great source of wall decor; many have a wide selection of prints, both framed and unframed. The black and white print *below left* has a contemporary feel with its wide white mat and slim metal frame. If you want it to have more prominence in a space—perhaps in a traditionally styled room—you may reframe it. The example *below right* has a custom-cut mat and frame, but lower-cost ready-mades are available at crafts and art supply stores for a similar look.

$102

$268

▶ **Sensible Shopper's Tip** Ask your favorite retailers where their leftover merchandise goes at the end of the season; many will steer you to a warehouse sale or outlet.

Who cares if no one but you wants a violet sofa? If you have a passion for purple, and a plain white room that needs a shot of color, that piece may be perfect for you. But before you buy such an offbeat item, ask yourself if you're really in love with it or if you just have a crush on the price. A purple sofa that turns into a white elephant a few weeks after it is delivered isn't a bargain: It's a bust.

Warehouse Wares and Discount Delights

If you don't mind wending your way through an overcrowded warehouse, shopping without sales help, and sometimes even transporting furniture home yourself, you should check out manufacturer warehouse sales. Sometimes these are held year-round in permanent buildings, called factory warehouses or outlets; other companies pitch tents and sell overstocks just one or two weekends a year.

Either way you can do very well on price if you're not overwhelmed by the crowded merchandise, and if you can check for product defects with eagle eyes. Because the pieces sold at warehouses and clearance centers may have been moved from location to location before you see them, they are more likely than pieces sold at retail to have minor (or even major) defects. And most of the time this merchandise is sold "as is." If you notice that dent or scratch after you pay for your purchase, you're out of luck—and potentially out of several hundred dollars. The bottom line: Look over pieces carefully for major flaws and open and close drawers to ensure they don't stick before you buy.

On Second Thought

If you live near an outlet mall or a manufacturers' headquarters, consider shopping for "seconds." If a product has a minor irregularity or damage, it can't be sold as a first-quality good. But often the "defect" doesn't affect the real value of the product in the slightest. For example, the bottom hem of a sheet might be slightly crooked—but if the hem of your sheet is always tucked in anyway, will you really care? Or perhaps that chair is marked as a second because it was supposed to have contrasting piping, but the factory accidentally left it off. If you like the chair just as much without the extra embellishment, this "second" can earn you first prize for sensible shopping.

Knockout Knockoffs

When you pay big bucks for designer-label pieces, you may be paying as much for the glamorous name as for the goods. Luckily many less elite manufacturers have no shame when it comes to duplicating the most expensive designer products—and these copycats can be terrific bargains. To get the best deal on knockoffs, shop the high-end retailers first. Write down

▶ Sensible Shopper's Tip Check out ethnic neighborhoods in your town or the nearest city. Almost every culture imports something to resell to locals, and the prices are usually very reasonable. Small shops that cater to immigrants are the best places to find Indian saris, Mexican rugs, or Turkish copper.

$30

$12.50

$110

The Look for Less

Knockoffs are an especially good way to save money on accessories, especially if you'll display them in a location where they might get damaged (such as on a table near a child's play space). Here are three pieces of pottery with very different price tags. The vessel *right* is from a New York City pottery manufacturer known for high-quality pieces with unique designs. You get the prestige of ownership—for $110. The two pieces *left* and *middle*, which have a similar look as the designer piece, are from a gift shop (*left*) and a reputable catalog (*right*)—and can be yours for a fraction of the price.

Garage—or tag—sales are a great place to hunt for bargains. For the best selection, arrive early, wear comfy clothes, and carry cash.

When a Bargain Isn't a Bargain

That flea market sofa is just the right size and shape for your living room, and even the cushions are in almost-like-new shape. And OK, so the pink and green pattern won't exactly go with your beige and bone living room, but you can always reupholster it, right? After all, the piece only costs $50. Hold it right there. Reupholstering a sofa can cost thousands of dollars; at that price, you're better off buying a brand-new sofa. When does it pay to reupholster? If your room requires an unusual size or shape sofa and you've just found it, or if the piece you love is an antique with a distinctive shape or profile, the cost of reupholstery is worth it; otherwise, look for a new sofa or a secondhand piece that looks just fine as is.

everything you can about a piece you love: the price, the dimensions, and special features or clues to quality. Then when you shop for look-alikes, you'll be able to evaluate whether you are really getting a fair deal or whether you'd be better off saving up for the "real thing."

Think Outside the Box

Sometimes the best buys are in the most unlikely places, so be sure to expand your hunt for home furnishings way beyond self-proclaimed home furnishings stores. Garden supply shops can be great sources of wicker and wrought-iron furnishings that look great indoors. Many clothing stores offer silk scarves that make great table toppers, as well as hair accessories you can use to stylishly tie back your drapes. And, for a surprising source of good-quality case goods at reasonable prices, check out stores that carry juvenile furnishings. Many chains and local children's furniture stores often sell basic dressers and armoires with ageless styling. The difference? The scale may be a bit smaller than "grown-up furniture," which actually makes these pieces perfect for small rooms or apartment living, and the prices are considerably lower than full-size pieces of comparable quality.

Insider Trading

You no longer have to be a professional designer to shop like one. Once open only to professional decorators, merchandise marts and manufacturer showrooms are increasingly accessible to the rest of us. In many major cities, "regular folks" can browse and shop at these designer meccas—often at a considerable discount. Check out the centers listed on page 187, which are now open (at select times) to the public. Call for rules, requirements, and hours.

Tag (Sale), You're It!

First the bad news: The days of finding an authentic 18th-century English dresser for $25 at a tag sale or scooping up a Picasso for pennies on someone's front lawn are long over. Information available on television and the Internet has created a whole new generation of savvier sellers, and it's unlikely that you'll find a million-dollar item for pocket change. Now the good news: Yard sales and flea markets can still yield terrific bargains. You may find not-quite-antique tables for less than $100 and dining chairs for much less than they'd cost new. And even when the prices are no lower than they would be at a chain store or discount sale, flea market finds often have the character and patina that newer pieces lack.

For the best selection at flea markets and yard sales, arrive early in the morning and, for the lowest prices, prepare to haggle a bit and pay in cash. Wear comfortable

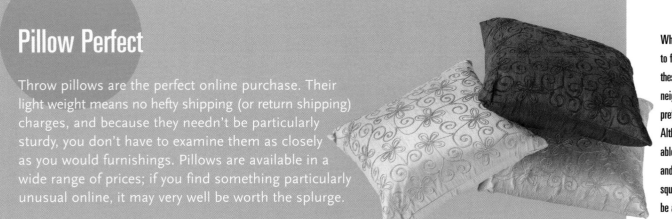

Pillow Perfect

Throw pillows are the perfect online purchase. Their light weight means no hefty shipping (or return shipping) charges, and because they needn't be particularly sturdy, you don't have to examine them as closely as you would furnishings. Pillows are available in a wide range of prices; if you find something particularly unusual online, it may very well be worth the splurge.

While you may be able to find pillows such as these in shops in your neighborhood, you may prefer to shop at home. Although you won't be able to feel the fabric and test pillows for squishiness, you may be able to find a great bargain online.

shoes and clothes that are easily cleaned if you get them dirty—and if possible leave your young children home. Flea market shopping can take lots of patience and a good deal of walking in less-than-perfect weather, and dragging an unwilling 3-year-old along can make for an unpleasant—and unproductive—day of shopping.

Classified Information

Homeowners who are looking to get rid of just a few pieces of furniture don't always bother holding a tag sale; instead, they often advertise in the classified ads. If you're looking for bargains on sofas, dining sets, or bookcases, check out your local newspaper and advertising circulars and look at Internet classifieds as well. Several major metropolitan areas now have virtual bulletin boards at www.Craigslist.com; updated daily, these listings provide a great source for everything from furniture to rugs.

Curb Appeal

Call it "dumpster diving" or "trolling for trash," but one of the best ways to score a bargain is to drive around a fancy

neighborhood the night before sanitation pickup day. You'd be amazed at what affluent homeowners leave out at the curb: end tables, wicker furniture, or even a perfectly serviceable sofa just sitting on the sidewalk waiting to be hauled away. Just check carefully to be sure that a family of squirrels hasn't taken up residence in that dresser. Then load the furniture into the back of your car or minivan and head on home. Total cost: a few dollars in gasoline.

Everything's On eBay

More than "just" a website, eBay is the world's biggest flea market and auction house, with countless products being offered for sale at any given time. Register for free at www.ebay.com, and you can bid on anything that strikes your fancy: vintage linens, designer furniture, upholstery fabrics, old postcards and maps, or fine-art photographs. There's plenty of mercury glass and McCoy pottery to be had, not to mention antique picture frames, brand-new lamps and chandeliers, name-brand dining sets and, well, you get the point. Just be careful: Not everything on eBay

is a bargain, so it's important to know what the item you're bidding on is really worth. If you find an item you like, be sure to check out the seller's feedback rating to confirm that he or she has delivered goods as promised to other customers, and ask any questions you may have about the item before you bid.

Everybody's Gone Surfin'

These days, it's possible to furnish your whole home without ever leaving it, thanks to the proliferation of home-decor websites and catalogs. And while you may not want to buy a sofa without sitting on it, or a bed without stretching out on it for at least a minute or two, the web and mail order are very convenient ways to find occasional tables, textiles, and accessories. (For buys that really are bargains, be sure to check a website or catalog's shipping charges and return policies before you order.) Websites also offer a good way to see what many bricks-and-mortar stores have to offer before you bother gassing up the car. See page 187 for some great ways to shop while you curl up with a cup of cocoa.

Sensibly Chic Projects

Designing a Sensibly Chic room with store-bought items is fun—you can mix and match furnishings and accessories from department and discount stores, tag sales, and beyond—and personalization comes from the way in which you combine your finds. But what if you can't find exactly what you want or, worse yet, you can't afford the item you've been dreaming about? That's when you'll want to invest your time and creativity in making these items yourself so you can complete your newly decorated space. Because nothing beats the sense of accomplishment you'll feel when you know you've done the work yourself, this section includes more than a dozen step-by-step projects and quick and easy embellishment ideas. It will show you how to add a personal touch to any room in your home in virtually no time at all.

Faux Leather Headboard

If you want a one-of-a-kind headboard, you are in luck: You can construct this custom unit in one day with readily available materials. When topped with detailed crown molding and embellished with a faux leather paint treatment and discount store photo frames, a humble piece of plywood becomes a stunning bedroom focal point.

You Will Need

8-foot length of 3x6 lumber

Birch plywood, cut 62x46"

6-foot length of crown molding

7-foot length of 1x3 lumber

8-foot length of lattice

Miter saw

15 5x7" photo frames, graph paper, pencil

Screws, nuts, bolts, small brads

Wood filler, putty knife, sandpaper, tack cloth

Screwdriver (cordless or manual), hammer

Primer, cream-color semigloss latex paint, brown semigloss latex paint (or other contrasting color), brown colored pencil, glazing medium

Paintbrushes, bucket, mixing tool, painter's tape, plastic wrap

Tape measure, ruler, T-square

Needle-nose pliers

Wood glue

Water-base polycrylic sealer

Cost: $250 Time: 1 day

This headboard is appropriate for a queen-size frame; use a piece of plywood sized to fit your specific bed frame; purchase molding and a 1x3 board to fit the width of the headboard.

ONE Cut the 3x6 in half (for two 3-foot-long pieces) and attach to the plywood as legs with screws. Space the legs 1 inch from the edges of the plywood; allow 10 inches of the legs to show at the bottom.

TWO Attach the crown molding to the top of the headboard, mitering the corners, to allow for a small mitered piece of crown molding to finish the edges. The crown molding should extend past the headboard on both ends, just enough to allow for the molding to be mitered and finished on the sides.

THREE Cut and attach the 1x3 to the top of the crown molding, allowing it to extend about 1 inch past the molding on each end. Cut the lattice piece in half and attach just below the crown molding, so that the pieces run vertically down and flush with the sides of the headboard. Fill all screw holes with wood filler, let dry, sand, and wipe away dust with a tack cloth.

FOUR Prime the entire headboard; let dry. Lightly sand and wipe with a tack cloth. Paint the headboard with the base coat; let dry.

FIVE Sketch the dimensions of the headboard and determine how you want the frames to be arranged on the headboard. When you are satisfied with the arrangement, use a tape measure or ruler and T-square and colored pencil to mark where each frame will be attached to the headboard.

SIX Using painter's tape, mark off each area to be painted (within each frame). Cut 15 pieces of plastic wrap, each 1 inch larger on all sides than the frame dimensions. Mix 4 parts glazing medium to 1 part contrasting color paint. Brush the mixture onto one masked-off area, press a piece of plastic wrap onto the just-painted surface, and peel away. Repeat the process for all masked-off areas; let dry.

SEVEN Remove the backing materials from the frames as well as any metal fastenings using needle-nose pliers. Sand each frame, wipe with a tack cloth, prime, and paint with the base coat; let dry.

EIGHT Using wood glue attach the frames to the headboard in the predetermined locations. If desired, tack the frames into place with small brads. Fill the nail holes with wood filler and touch up with paint as needed; let dry.

NINE Apply two coats of polycrylic sealer to the entire headboard, allowing it to dry between coats.

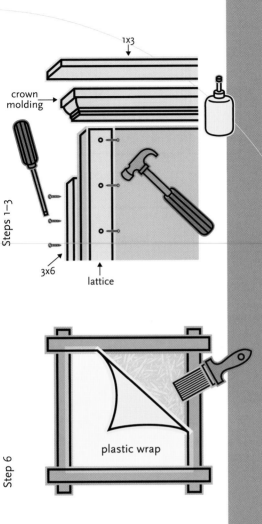

1x3

crown molding

Steps 1–3

3x6

lattice

plastic wrap

Step 6

Graphic Ribbon Pillow

Sometimes a simple design has the most impact, as this pillow proves: Three rows of layered ribbons are stitched to a pillow front in a uniform design. The gray, powder blue, and vibrant green used for this pillow make a contemporary statement, but you can create a different look altogether by using different colors.

You Will Need

1 yard pillow fabric, gray or other desired color

1½", ⅞", ⅜" satin ribbon in green, blue, and gray (or other desired colors)

Scissors, tape measure, sewing machine, thread in colors that match ribbons, straight pins, vanishing fabric marker, monofilament thread

10x14" pillow form

Cost: $25 Time: 3 hours

Finished pillow size is 20½x17".

ONE Cut two pieces from the pillow fabric, each measuring 21x17½ inches.

TWO Determine the color order of the three ribbon units for the pillow top, layering the ribbons from widest to narrowest. When you are satisfied with the color combination, cut all ribbons 21 inches long. Note: To prevent the ribbon ends from fraying, you may use a wood-burning tool and nonmelting cutting surface; see page 173 for more information.

THREE Pin the three layered ribbon units to the right side of one piece of the cut pillow fabric (this will be the pillow top); the top and bottom units should be placed approximately 5 inches from the raw edge of the pillow top, and the middle unit should be placed between the top and bottom, approximately 1¾ inches from each. Using thread that matches the top (narrow) ribbon, stitch the ribbon units in place, starting and stopping 3½ inches from the ribbon ends (so that they will hang freely).

FOUR Put the pillow top and backing fabric right sides together. Stitch around three sides of the pillow using a ¼-inch seam allowance, ensuring none of the free-hanging ribbons becomes stitched in the seam. Turn the pillow right side out.

FIVE Measure and mark a line 3½ inches from each edge of the pillow. Pin the pillow top and backing together and stitch along the marked line, stitching under the free-hanging ribbons and leaving an opening that aligns with the outer edge opening.

SIX Insert the pillow form into the pillow. Push the pillow form away from the pillow cover opening and stitch along the line marked in Step 5 to enclose the pillow form and complete the flange edge.

SEVEN Slip-stitch the opening at the outer edge closed with the monofilament thread. Fluff the pillow to evenly distribute the pillow form in the center portion.

Step 3

3½"

Step 5

3½"

Leave bottom edge open; stitch closed in Step 6.

Exotic Faux Suede Pillow

Soft and luxurious best describe faux suede, making it the perfect fabric for cushy pillows just right for a bed or sofa. This pillow—with its contemporary square-within-a-square motif—has minimal stitching because most of the pieces are glued into place (faux suede doesn't ravel).

You Will Need

Faux suede: 1/3 yard animal print, 1/4 yard black, 1/2 yard brown (or other desired colors)

Rotary cutter, self-healing cutting mat, ruler, 45-degree triangle ruler

Clear-drying fabric adhesive

Sewing machine, straight pins, black thread

Polyester stuffing

Cost: $35 Time: 4 hours

Finished pillow size is 18x18".

ONE Using the rotary cutter and self-healing cutting mat, cut the faux suede as follows: two pieces 18x18 inches, brown; 3-inch square and four strips 13x2¹/₂ inches, animal print; four strips 1x6 inches and four strips 1x16 inches, black. Using the 45-degree triangle, miter the corners of each strip of fabric (so that they will come together in a frame).

Faux Suede

Man-made faux suede is available in a wide array of solid colors and prints—and even embroidered with various designs—so you are sure to find just the right combination that will complement your decorating scheme. The highest quality faux suede may cost up to $60 per yard, but good-quality fabrics can be found for as little as $15 per yard. Faux suede is considerably more expensive than most cottons typically used for pillows, but when you want a hint of luxury, supple faux suede can't be beat.

TWO Choose one piece of brown fabric as the pillow front. Find the exact center and glue the 3" square of animal-print fabric in place; let dry.

THREE Measure ¹/₂ inch from the animal-print square and glue the four mitered pieces of 1x6 black fabric around the square; let dry.

FOUR Measure ⁷/₈ inch from the black mitered strips and glue the four mitered pieces of 13x2¹/₂-inch animal-print fabric in place; let dry.

FIVE Measure ¹/₂ inch from the animal-print mitered strips and glue the four mitered pieces of 1x16-inch black fabric in place; let dry.

SIX Stack the pillow top and backing fabric right sides together. Stitch around three sides of the pillow, 1³/₄ inches from the edge, creating a flange edge. Note: When you turn the pillow right side out, the stitch should dissect the outermost black strips in half. Turn the pillow right side out, fill with polyester stuffing, and machine-stitch the opening closed 1³/₄ from the edge.

⁷/₈" ¹/₂"

¹/₂"

Steps 1–5

Step 6

Stitch through the outermost strips to create the flange edge.

Crazy Quilt Pillow

At the end of the 19th century—when accessories for the home, clothing, and beyond were highly decorated—crazy quilts became popular. These quilts are characterized by irregular-size patches in nearly every color and pattern of fabric and intricate hand stitching between the patches. This fun pillow is a simple interpretation of this classic quilt design: The patches are stitched together, and craft store trims take the place of elaborate hand stitches.

You Will Need

1/4 yard brushed velvet, mauve and black (or other desired colors)

1/2 yard brushed velvet for backing fabric, black (or other desired color)

Trims and ribbons, white (or various colors)

Scissors, tape measure

Sewing machine, straight pins, hand-sewing needle, thread that matches pillow backing, monofilament thread

Fray-preventing liquid

Clear-drying fabric adhesive

Polyester stuffing

Cost: $25 Time: 4 hours

Finished pillow size is 17x14".

What Is a Slip Stitch?

A slip stitch is commonly used to join a folded edge to a flat piece of fabric or two folded edges, as is the case with this pillow. Because this stitch is formed by slipping the needle and thread under a fold, it is nearly invisible on the right side of a project.

1. Starting at the left side, fold the open edge of the pillow front ¼ inch to the inside; insert the needle into the fold and hide a knot inside the hem.

2. Fold the edge of the pillow back ¼ inch to the inside; insert the needle into the folded edge and pull the thread through.

3. Continue slipping the needle through the folded edges, alternating between the pillow front and backing fabric.

ONE Cut the velvet into irregular shapes (i.e., lopsided squares and triangles) and lay them flat on your work space to see how the pieces will appear once sewn, allowing a ¼-inch seam all around each piece. Stitch the pieces together to create a pillow top that measures 18x15 inches.

TWO Lay pieces of ribbon and trim over the joins of the velvet shapes. Once you have a pleasing design cut the ribbons and trims and dip the edges into the fray-preventing liquid; let dry.

THREE Glue the trims to the pillow top in the predetermined locations; let dry.

FOUR For the pillow back, cut a piece of fabric that measures 18x15 inches. Stack the pillow top and backing fabric right sides together; stitch with a ½-inch seam allowance. Turn the pillow right side out, insert the polyester stuffing, and slip-stitch the opening closed with the monofilament thread.

Allow a ¼-inch seam around each piece.

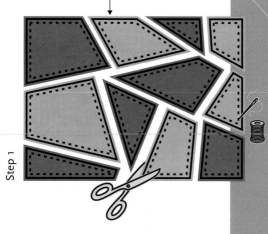

Step 1

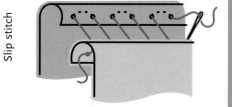

Slip stitch

Sensibly Chic Embellishment Techniques

Sometimes the easiest way to get a fresh new look is to add some pizzazz to a ready-made object. This saves you the time of creating an item from scratch—and allows you to put your creativity into the personalization. Fast, fun, and fresh best describe this collection of ideas. Use these examples as a springboard to add a dash of color or a dose of print to any humdrum item.

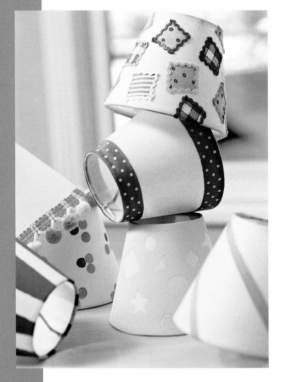

Light My Way **Inexpensive plain paper or fabric lampshades with a nonglossy finish offer the perfect embellishment opportunity! From the top, clockwise:**

ONE Cut 1-inch fabric squares and adhere them to the shade in a random fashion with clear-drying tacky glue. Frame each fabric square with rickrack trim.

TWO Cut 2 pieces of ribbon: one 1 inch longer than the circumference of the upper edge of the shade, one 1 inch longer than the circumference of the lower edge. Using a hot-glue gun adhere the ribbon to the shade, turning the end under $1/2$ inch to conceal the raw edge.

THREE Apply removable stickers of any desired shape to the shade. Paint the shade with acrylic paint (use as many coats as needed to completely cover the shade); let dry. Carefully remove the stickers.

FOUR Using a pencil and tape measure, divide the shade into even increments along the top and bottom edges. Hot-glue strips of $5/8$-inch-wide grosgrain ribbon from one point to another, forming diagonal lines. Glue excess ribbon to the inside of the shade at the top and bottom edges.

FIVE Mask off evenly spaced stripes with painter's tape of any desired width. Paint the exposed areas of the shade with acrylic paint (use as many coats as needed to completely cover the shade); let dry. Carefully remove the tape.

SIX Apply clusters of preinked mini-stamps to the shade; let dry.

SEVEN Cut ball fringe 1 inch longer than the circumference of the lower edge of the shade. Hot-glue the fringe to the shade, allowing the balls to hang below the rim. Turn the end under $1/2$ inch to conceal the raw edge.

Sleep Easy

Sleep Easy Stencil your way to a good night's sleep with this easy-to-embellish bedding. The letter z is used in the example, but use the alphabet for cute kids' bedding or an inviting message for a guest room.

ONE Select letters in the desired fonts on a computer; enlarge and print. Note: The letters shown range from $4^1/_2$ to $13^1/_2$ inches high. Follow the instructions on page 179 for making stencils.

TWO Lay the bedding on a large, flat surface right side up. Insert a large plastic sheet or piece of cardboard under the bedding or between pillow layers. Using painter's tape adhere the stencils to the bedding.

THREE Mix 2 parts acrylic paint with 1 part textile medium. Use a stencil brush to fill in the letters; let dry. Remove the stencils and heat-set the bedding following the textile medium manufacturer's directions.

Pattern Perfect

Pattern Perfect **A combination of paint and decoupage papers, which are available at crafts and art supply stores as well as on the Internet in nearly every color and motif imaginable, can turn even the most ordinary piece of furniture into a work of art.**

ONE Remove the doors and drawers from the piece of furniture, if necessary, as well as any hardware. Paint the furnishing in the desired color(s) with flat-finish latex paint; let dry.

TWO Cut the decoupage paper motifs using sharp scissors. Arrange the motifs on the piece of furniture until you are pleased with the placement.

THREE Apply decoupage medium to the back of the motifs using a foam brush or paintbrush and adhere in the predetermined locations. Wipe away excess decoupage medium with a damp sponge and use a wallpaper brush or rigid plastic card to seal the edges of the motifs. After all motifs are placed, coat the entire project with two to three thin, even coats of decoupage medium, allowing it to dry between coats.

FOUR Reassemble the piece of furniture, if needed.

Decoupaged Storage Ottoman

Take a walk on the wild side with a toy chest decoupaged with animal-print tissue paper. Add a padded top and some coordinating fabric, and the toy chest becomes a trendy ottoman that offers storage space and seating for any room in your home.

You Will Need

Ready-to-assemble (RTA) toy chest in maple or other light wood finish

Ruler and pencil

Animal-print decorative and tissue paper, coordinating solid colors of tissue paper

Matte-finish decoupage medium, disposable foam brushes

Water-base polycrylic sealer

½"-thick upholstery foam

Serrated knife

Hot-glue gun and glue sticks

Animal-print canvas 4" wider and 4" longer than the chest top

Staple gun and staples

Coordinating solid-color fabric the same size as the chest top

Awl, screwdriver or cordless drill

Crafts knife

Cost: $75   Time: 4 hours

ONE Do not assemble the chest. Set the top aside; you will not decoupage it. Work on each piece separately, completing it before moving on to the next piece. Before applying any decoupage medium or paper, measure the location of all predrilled holes; mark the position of these holes on the chest's assembly instructions (this will allow you to locate these holes after they are covered with paper and make assembly of the chest easier).

TWO Tear the decorative and tissue paper into small (approximately 4x8-inch) irregular-shape pieces. Starting with one section of the chest, apply a thin, even layer of decoupage medium. Begin to lay pieces of the decorative and tissue paper onto the wet medium, smoothing the paper in place to reduce wrinkles and applying additional medium over the edges of the paper pieces to ensure they stay flat. Be sure to wrap the tissue paper around the edges and to the other side. Repeat until the entire piece is covered with several layers of tissue paper. Let all pieces dry. Apply a thin, even layer of decoupage medium over all pieces; let dry.

THREE Cover all pieces with two coats of water-base polycrylic sealer, allowing the sealer to dry between coats.

FOUR Hot-glue the foam to the chest top to tack it in place. Using a serrated knife, cut the foam even with the edges of the chest top.

FIVE Place the canvas right side down on your work surface. Center the foam-covered top facedown on the canvas. Wrap the fabric to the back side of the top so it is taut but not distorted. Place a single staple in the center of each side, near the raw edge of the fabric. Working from the center staple, staple the fabric all around. Fold the corners into a miter and staple them in place.

SIX Finger-press a 1-inch hem on all sides of the coordinating fabric. Center it over the back of the chest top so it conceals the raw, stapled edges of the canvas. Staple the fabric lining in place.

SEVEN Referring to the marks made in Step 1, use an awl to carefully locate all predrilled holes. Punch through the paper or fabric so the holes are accessible. Assemble the chest according to the manufacturer's directions. If desired, use a crafts knife to trim away any paper that shows on the inside of the chest. Reseal any trimmed edges with two additional coats of decoupage medium.

Step 2

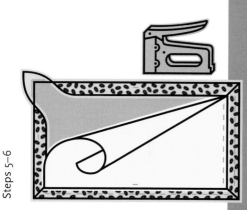

Steps 5–6

Sophisticated Chair Slipcover

Give an old dining chair a new lease on life with a tailored slipcover that's surprisingly easy to make! This fitted slipcover is topped with a sheer removable covering on the seat that skims the floor like a graceful ballroom skirt. In the example shown a purple fabric with a meandering floral design is used for the slipcover, while a delicately striped fabric covers the seat for a fun mix of pattern and texture. Feel free to play with different colors, patterns, and textures of fabric for a fresh, personalized look.

After

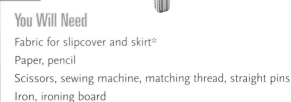

Before

You Will Need

Fabric for slipcover and skirt*
Paper, pencil
Scissors, sewing machine, matching thread, straight pins
Iron, ironing board

Cost: $35 Time: 4 hours

*A heavy cotton was used for this slipcover, while a sheer fabric was used for the skirt. Purchase fabric for this project after measuring the chair.

ONE Start at the lower back edge of the chair (where a leg meets the floor) and measure up and over the back of the chair and across the seat to the front edge of the seat (A). Add 3 inches for the back hem and ½ inch for the seam on the front edge. Measure the width of the chair seat and back at their narrowest and widest points and their lengths (B), adding 1 inch for seam allowances. Measure the slipcover skirt length from the seat edge to the floor (C). Add 3 inches for the hem and ½ inch for the seam at the seat. To measure the slipcover skirt width, start at one back leg and wrap the tape measure around all legs (D). Add 1 inch for the seam on each edge. Record all measurements.

TWO Cut all slipcover fabrics using the measurements determined in Step 1. Press all hems on the slipcover skirt pieces. Pin the pieces, wrong side out, together over the chair to check the fit. Stitch all hems and stitch the pieces together using a ½-inch seam allowance.

THREE For the sheer skirt overlay, use the measurements for the seat and skirt recorded in Step 1, but add only 1 inch to the skirt for the hem and double the skirt width measurement to allow for pleats at the front and back corners.

FOUR Hem the long edge of the sheer skirt overlay and the back edge of the seat. Pin the seat and overlay pieces to the chair, starting at center front and making 3-inch pleats at the front corners; pin the pleats in place. Continue wrapping the skirt around the chair and make 3-inch pleats at the back corners; pin in place. Remove from the chair and stitch the skirt to the seat on three sides, leaving the back hemmed edge open. Press a narrow hem at the back open edge; topstitch the hem.

Step 1

Step 3

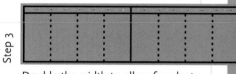

Double the width to allow for pleats.

Step 4

Custom Roller Shade

A readily available kit makes it easy to turn classic decorator fabric into a fashionable window shade. You can embellish the shade with trims and tassels for a one-of-a-kind look. The best part? No sewing is required!

You Will Need

Light- to medium-weight fabric for the shade, 12" longer than the window length, in any color or pattern

Roller shade kit

Pencil, yardstick

Rotary cutter and self-healing mat or scissors

Upholstery braid and tassel, both in colors that complement the shade fabric

Clear-drying fabric adhesive

Thread in color that matches the tassel, needle

Fray-preventing liquid

Cost: $30 Time: 3 hours

Project Option: Easy-Stitch Valance

If you want to add a little more pizzazz to your roller shade, top it with a flat valance in matching or complementary fabric.

1. Cut the valance fabric 2 inches wider than the roller shade and 13 inches long.

2. Turn under both side edges 1/2 inch, then another 1/2 inch, encasing the raw edges. Topstitch along the fold lines.

3. Turn the upper and lower edges of the valance under 1/2 inch, then 1 1/2 inches to create a rod pocket. Topstitch along the fold lines.

4. Press the valance and insert tension rods in the upper and lower casings for a taut valance.

ONE Following the roller shade kit instructions, cut the shade backing and shade fabric to size using the rotary cutter and self-healing mat or scissors. Fuse the two materials together. If desired, insert a pull slat in the shade and shape the lower edge.

TWO Cut the upholstery braid in a length (or lengths) required to cover the lower edge of the shade. Glue the upholstery braid to the shade. Hand-stitch the tassel in place as a shade pull. To prevent fraying, treat the side edges with fray-preventing liquid. Let the glue and fray-preventing liquid dry completely.

THREE Assemble the shade according to the kit instructions.

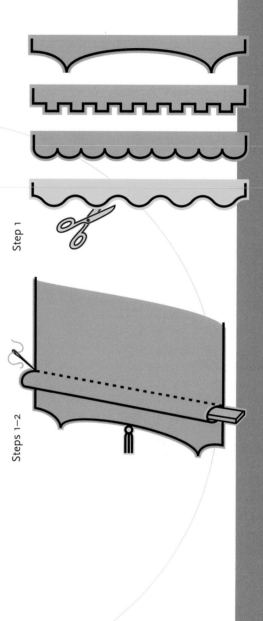

Step 1

Steps 1–2

Tips for Success

Shade kits come with easy-to-use instructions, but follow these tips for hassle-free project completion:

▶ **Work on a large, smooth surface such as a floor or table.** When ironing, place a folded bedsheet under the shade to protect the work surface. Do not work on an ironing board or a padded surface.

▶ **Before cutting the shade backing and shade fabric, make sure the pieces are perfectly aligned.** If they are not straight and square, the pattern will become distorted when applied to the shade.

▶ **When fusing the backing to the fabric, set the fused length over a table or another surface.** Allowing the fused fabric to hang over the edge of the work surface may break the freshly fused bond or cause the remaining fabric to become off-center.

Woven Ribbon Window Treatment

If you are dreaming of a romantic, shimmery window treatment—and you don't want to sew—this project is for you! Just purchase a window panel with a rod pocket in a color that complements your decor, weave a rainbow of ribbons, attach them to the panel, and voilá: You have a beautiful way to frame your favorite view. One panel, which is tied back with a single piece of sheer ribbon, is shown, but repeat the instructions for as many panels as you desire.

You Will Need

Sheer ribbon in various widths and a variety of colors

1/4"-wide satin ribbon in color that matches window panel

Scissors or wood-burning tool (see page 173 for more information)

Large piece of foam-core board, straight pins

Clear-drying fabric adhesive

Window panel(s) with rod pocket in the desired color

Small safety pins

Cost: $30 Time: 3 hours

ONE Cut 25 pieces of varying widths of ribbons, each 70 inches long. Cut 33 pieces of varying widths of ribbons, each 32 inches long. Note: The window panel shown is 5½ feet long and 2½ feet wide; adjust the length and width of the woven ribbon unit—and the number of ribbons used—if your panel is shorter or longer.

TWO Attach the 70-inch-long pieces of ribbon to the piece of foam-core board using straight pins, leaving approximately 2 inches loose at the top.

THREE Starting just under the secured pieces of ribbon, take one piece of 32-inch-long ribbon and weave it through the 70-inch-long pieces, going over and under each alternating piece. Leave about 2 inches loose on each end. Repeat this process, alternating the pieces, until the ribbon unit is 12 inches long (in this example, 11 pieces of ribbon were used).

FOUR Remove the straight pins from the ribbon unit. Cut a 32-inch piece of satin ribbon and secure to the top of the ribbon unit with fabric adhesive; let dry.

FIVE To secure the ribbons, place drops of fabric adhesive to the top, sides, and bottom of the ribbon unit; let dry.

Remove the ribbon unit from the foam-core board and carefully reposition it so that the next row to be woven starts about 10 inches below the first woven section; secure with straight pins. Repeat the weaving and gluing process until you have a unit that is 5½ feet long (or the length needed to cover approximately three-quarters the length of your window panel).

SIX Trim the ribbons, leaving approximately 1 inch loose on each side and 10 inches on the bottom.

SEVEN Center the ribbon unit on top of the window panel; fold the top of the unit (where the satin ribbon is attached) over the rod pocket and attach to the back of the window panel with small safety pins. Allow the sides and bottom of the ribbon unit to hang freely.

Cutting Ribbon with a Wood-Burning Tool

To prevent ribbon ends from fraying, use a wood-burning tool to cut the ribbons. Use caution when working with a wood-burning tool because it will be very hot. Also note that you will need a nonmelting cutting surface and a metal ruler for cutting straight lines.

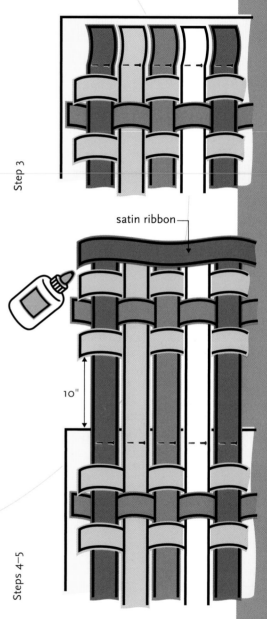

Step 3

satin ribbon

10"

Steps 4–5

Sensibly Chic No-Sew Window Treatments

Dressing your windows in style doesn't need to cost a fortune, as these stylish examples prove. By using ready-made items in innovative ways, you can create wow factor in any room in your home.

Scarf Style

Create this simple—yet impactful—treatment in a jiffy with a long silk scarf and earring hooks.

ONE Hand-stitch the earring hooks on one long edge of the scarf. Note: This scarf is 95 inches long; the hooks are attached 25 inches from each end to allow the ends to drape once hung.

TWO Fasten wall hooks into the window trim. To allow for a slight drape when the scarf is hung, place the wall hooks 2 inches closer than the distance between the earring hooks on the scarf. Slip the earring hooks on the wall hooks.

Tablecloth Trick

Discount and department stores abound with tablecloths in a wide range of colors, motifs, and styles that can beautify your dining space. But, tablecloths can also serve as stylish curtain panels.

ONE Cut approximately 15 inches from the top of each tablecloth (in the example shown the tablecloths measure 55x100 inches; purchase sizes to fit your window height).

TWO Lay one panel right side down; place the 15-inch cut portion (the valance) on top of it right side down with the raw top edges matching. Pin and sew along the raw top edge using a $1/2$-inch seam allowance. Flip the valance to the right side of the panel; press. Topstitch through all layers $1/2$ inch from the seam. Repeat this process for the other panel.

THREE Attach curtain rings to the top edge of each panel and slip the rings over a curtain rod.

Beaded Beauty

Light-catching beads offer a quick way to fashionably embellish a pretty window treatment alone. Looking for a suite of projects? Use beads to dress up other accents, such as lampshades and pillows.

ONE Hem the top and bottom edges of a piece of 45-inch-wide cotton voile fabric ($2^{1}/_{2}$ yards were used to cover this window) with narrow rolled hems.

TWO Make beaded strands by threading a needle and sliding on one bead; knot. Thread enough beads onto each strand to make them $2^{1}/_{2}$ inches long. Trim both ends of the panel with a beaded border, spacing the beaded strands evenly across the fabric and fastening the strands to the hem of the cotton voile.

THREE Hang the curtain by slipping it over a tension rod, gathering it slightly and pulling it at an angle.

Contemporary Wood Block Lamp

You can easily find most of the materials for this lamp—that's worthy of display in a gallery—in a home center. If the bright paint colors shown in this example don't suit your decor, substitute any color combination you prefer, stain the wood for just a hint of color, or leave the blocks raw for an industrial look.

You Will Need

4-foot length of 2x4, pencil, ruler, saw

Wooden plaque, approximately 6³/₄" square

Drill or drill press and ⁷/₁₆" or ¹/₂" drill bit and screwdriver bit

Sandpaper, tack cloth

Disposable foam brushes, acrylic paint in purple, fuchsia, yellow, blue, and orange (or other desired colors)

Chrome-color spray paint

30" long threaded lamp pipe (also called all-thread pipe), hacksaw

Four 1¹/₄" plate-backed caster wheels, awl, hammer, ¹/₂" flat-head screws

2 lock nuts

Lamp-making kit with neck, cord, and socket

Purchased square lampshade

Cost: $50   Time: 3 hours

ONE Cut the 2x4 into eleven 3½-inch-long pieces. Mark the center of each piece and the center of the plaque. Drill through all the pieces. Sand the pieces, breaking the edges slightly, and wipe away any dust with a tack cloth.

TWO Paint two pieces with each of the five paint colors. Use two or more coats, sanding lightly between each coat. Paint the remaining 2x4 piece and the plaque with chrome spray paint.

THREE Stack the blocks on the plaque in a pleasing order, with the chrome-color block in the center. Slip the lamp pipe through the center holes. Place a lock nut on the end under the plaque. Screw the lamp neck onto the pipe so it is firmly against the top block. Measure ½ inch above the top of the neck and mark the pipe at that point. Remove the neck and pipe from the blocks and plaque. Thread a second lock nut ½ inch below the marking. Using a hacksaw, cut through the lamp pipe at the marking. Thread the lock nut over the cut and off the pipe. This will remove any burrs left from cutting and make it easier to screw the socket in place.

FOUR Turn the plaque upside down. Place the wheels on the plaque so the plate backs are positioned ½ inch in from all edges. Mark the screw openings of the plates, then remove the wheels. Make a pilot hole at each mark using an awl and hammer. Put the wheels in place and screw them to the plaque.

FIVE Turn the plaque upright, slide the pipe up through the hole, and put the blocks back into place. Thread the lamp neck onto the top end of the pipe. Turn the blocks as desired, then tighten both the lower lock nut and the neck. Slide the cord through the pipe and assemble the socket as described in the lamp-making kit instructions. If the shade requires a harp, add the harp base when assembling the socket.

SIX Spray-paint the shade with several coats of chrome-color paint until the shade is completely covered and the paint is even; let dry. If desired, lightly spray the inside of the shade. Place the shade on the lamp base.

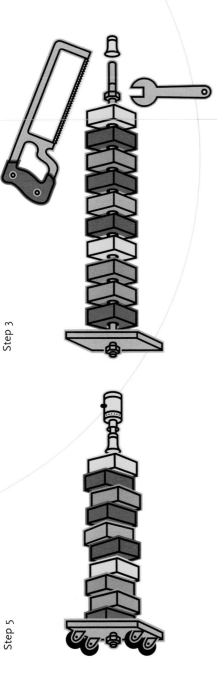

Step 3

Step 5

Tropical Stenciled Rug

Bring the feeling of an exotic locale into your home with this easy-to-stencil sisal rug. You can make stencils yourself using the patterns provided, or look at arts or crafts stores for a wide array of ready-made stencils in similar designs.

palm frond

Enlarge motifs to a size that complements the size and shape of your rug.

coconut

You Will Need

Sisal rug with fabric-covered edge*

Small triangular foam stamp, cosmetic sponge

Premade palm frond and coconut stencils (or materials to make stencils yourself; see page 179)

Stencil spray adhesive

Wax-base stencil paints in green, brown, black

Stencil brushes, one for each color of paint

Rag, paper towels

Cost: $150 Time: 4 hours

***The rug used in the project shown is 5x8 feet.**

ONE Using the cosmetic sponge, apply some of the brown stencil paint to the foam stamp. Randomly stamp a design on the fabric-covered edge of the rug. Using a stencil brush, apply the brown paint to the outer and inner edges of the fabric border.

TWO Place the palm frond stencil on one corner of the rug; when you are satisfied with its placement, spray stencil adhesive on the back of the stencil and press onto the rug. Following the manufacturer's instructions, apply the green paint to the stencil openings with a pouncing motion; let dry.

THREE Clean the stencil; dry. Flip the stencil over and stencil the palm frond in the corner opposite the design created in Step 2 (so that the fronds are mirror images of each other). Repeat the stenciling process in Step 2.

Making Stencils

1. Draw or trace the desired motif onto paper. Transfer the design to translucent stencil plastic: Place the pattern underneath the plastic and trace with a fine-tip marker.

2. Using a self-healing cutting mat, cut out the stenciled designs with a crafts knife.

FOUR Repeat Steps 2 and 3 for the remaining two corners of the rug.

FIVE Determine how many coconuts you want on each side of the rug (between the palm fronds). In the rug shown five coconuts are stenciled on the long sides and three coconuts are stenciled on the shorter ends; the coconuts are slightly staggered for a free-form feel. (**Note:** You can alternate the size of the coconuts if desired or use all coconuts of the same size.) Once you have determined the number of coconuts you would like, spray the back of the coconut stencil with spray adhesive. Using the brown stencil paint, stencil the coconut, leaving the middle portion unpainted; use more paint toward the outer edges of the design and less paint toward the inside of the design for a shadow effect. Define the outer portion of the coconut using the black stencil paint. Remove the stencil and use the brush to paint a freehand circle in the desired location for the stem.

SIX Repeat Step 5 to stencil the remaining coconuts.

SEVEN Allow rug to cure for 10 days before using.

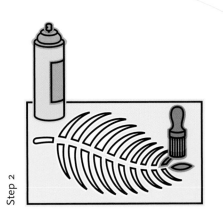

Step 2

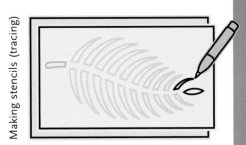

Making stencils (tracing)

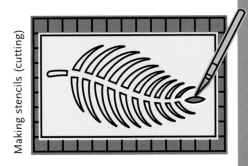

Making stencils (cutting)

Classy Photo Frame

For this easy, elegant frame, wide grosgrain ribbon resembles photo corners, often used in albums and scrapbooks. It's wrapped around two pieces of glass. Black is used to complement this vintage photograph, but let your chosen photograph and its subject matter determine the color or pattern of ribbon for your frame.

You Will Need

2 pieces of framing glass*

Protective gloves, sandpaper, tack cloth

Glass cleaner, paper towels

Photo of your choice

Optional: Photo corners

Foam photo mounting squares, scissors

Flat photo hangers

2¼" wide grosgrain ribbon, black (or color of your choice)

⅛" wide satin ribbon, black (or color of your choice)

Clear-drying adhesive

Cost: $25 Time: 1 hour

*You can purchase this glass at a hardware or framing store; most retailers will cut the glass free of charge or for a minimal fee. The glass used in this project is 9x10", but determine the size for your frame after you choose a photograph.

FOUR Turn the piece of glass with the mounted photo faceup. Place mounting foam in the four corners of the glass piece. Remove the paper backing from the mounting foam and carefully place the remaining piece of glass on top, aligning all edges.

FIVE Cut two 24-inch lengths of satin ribbon; thread one ribbon through each photo hanger.

SIX Wrap grosgrain ribbon around one corner of the frame unit to determine the length required to completely cover the corner and be secured to the back of the frame. Cut the ribbon to the determined length; use this measurement to cut three additional pieces. Wrap one piece of ribbon around each corner; secure with glue and let dry.

SEVEN Tie the satin ribbons in a knot or bow and hang.

ONE While wearing gloves, sand the edges of the glass for a smooth finish. Wipe away any dust with a tack cloth. Clean both sides of each glass piece with glass cleaner and paper towels.

TWO If desired, attach photo corners to your photograph. Adhere the photo to the center of one piece of glass using foam mounting squares (cut the foam pieces small enough so that you cannot see them once the photo is attached).

THREE Turn the piece of glass with the mounted photo facedown. Place the flat photo hangers in the top two corners so that the loops are near the corners. Secure the hangers to the glass with mounting foam.

Step 5

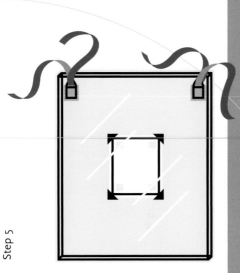

Step 6

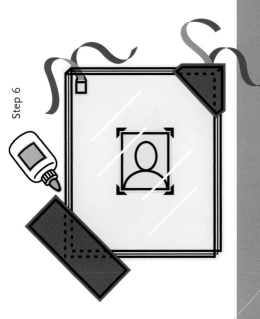

Metal-Covered Frame

Part sleek and chic, part rustic and rough, this metal-covered frame is the perfect way to showcase cherished family photographs or colorful prints. The combination of aluminum and nickel upholstery tacks is very streamlined, but you can also mix things up a bit by using brass or black-color tacks.

You Will Need

Photo frame with flat frame*
Paper and pencil
Aluminum sheets
Scissors, tin snips
Staple gun, staples
Burnishing tool, such as
    a wood craft stick
Nickel upholstery tacks**
Hammer
Wood skewer

Cost: $25 Time: 2 hours

*The frame used for this project
has an opening for a 8x10" photo
with a flat 1½" wide x ¾" deep frame.
**When purchasing upholstery tacks
select a nailhead width that will
evenly divide into the frame perimeter.

ONE Remove the back, cardboard insert, and glass from the frame. Trace the frame onto the paper, adding an allowance for the frame depth and extra for wrapping and securing the metal to the frame; cut out. Trace the pattern on the aluminum sheet; cut out using tin snips. **Note:** You may need to piece the aluminum together to make a complete pattern.

TWO Place the aluminum on the front of the frame. Make small cuts in the corners of the aluminum where it will wrap around the frame edges. Wrap the aluminum around the frame, using a burnishing tool to smooth. Staple the aluminum to the back of the frame.

THREE Pound an upholstery tack into one corner of the frame. Continue pounding tacks into the frame, spacing them evenly around the perimeter of the frame until you return to the starting point.

FOUR To distress the frame, gently pound the end of the wood skewer onto the exposed aluminum in a random fashion.

Alternate Materials

If you are unable to find aluminum sheets at a crafts or art supply store, try these alternatives:

- **Metal flashing** from a home center.
- **Craft foil,** available in a rainbow of colors.
- **Heavyweight** fabric.

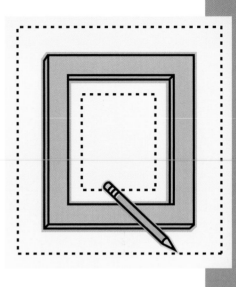

Step 1

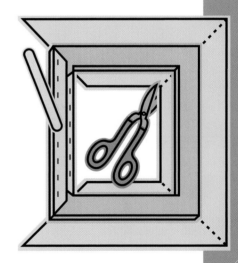

Step 2

Sensibly Chic Finishes

Embellishing the surface of a furnishing or accessory—with paint, stain, and even glizty gold or silver leaf—is one of the easiest ways to get the most bang for your decorating buck. These techniques offer an economical way to revitalize thrift store or flea market finds and personalize new, unfinished furnishings that often cost significantly less than their prefinished cousins.

Pretty in Paint Adding a distressed paint finish is an easy way to enhance any piece of furniture, old and new alike, kitchen cabinets, or any wood surface. Distressing a piece gives it old, rustic charm perfect for rooms decorated in nearly any style (especially a relaxed cottage space). For this technique you will choose two paint colors; the base coat will be seen only where the top coat is sanded away. If you select a piece of vintage furniture to distress, ensure it is sturdy and in good condition prior to painting (taking minor repairs into consideration if you have the skills and budget to allow for them).

ONE Prime the project surface; let dry. Lightly sand the project surface and wipe away any dust with a tack cloth.

TWO Apply a base coat in the desired color to the project surface; let dry. Apply a top coat in the desired color; let dry.

THREE Sand any raised areas of the surface (where natural wear would occur), rubbing away portions of the top coat paint and revealing the base coat beneath. Wipe away any dust with a tack cloth.

FOUR If desired, randomly brush water-base stain onto one area of the project surface; quickly wipe away some of the stain with a lint-free cloth, allowing it to sink into any recessed areas for an aged appearance. Continue applying and wiping away the stain until the entire surface has been covered.

FIVE Apply two coats of water-base polycrylic to the entire surface, allowing it to dry between coats.

Simply Stained
Wood stains, available in many wood tones as well as fashion colors—such as blues, greens, and oranges—offer cost-effective opportunities to beautify any wood surface. For safety's sake use water-base stains, which do not produce hazardous fumes like oil-base (alkyd) stains. However, always work in a well-ventilated area and wear rubber gloves to protect your hands.

ONE If desired, apply wood conditioner to the project surface prior to staining; this will encourage an even appearance (many soft woods, such as pine, have uneven grains that result in irregular absorption, so the finished appearance may be blotchy).

TWO Use a lint-free cloth to apply the stain to the surface. Use long, continuous strokes and apply the stain to small areas of the project surface at a time. For best results apply the stain in the same direction as the wood grain. Wipe the wet stain with another lint-free cloth to remove excess stain and ensure an even coat; let dry. Reapply the stain if a darker finish is desired.

THREE Apply two coats of water-base polycrylic to the project surface, allowing it to dry between coats.

Lovely Leafing
Metallic leaf, microthin sheets of metallic composition metal, offers an affordable way to get the expensive look of gold, silver, or copper on nearly any project surface without spending a lot of green. Look for leafing kits with all the supplies you need at art supply and crafts stores.

ONE Thoroughly clean the project surface. Seal the surface with gesso.

TWO Apply adhesive to the project surface, following the manufacturer's instructions.

THREE Cut pieces of waxed paper larger than the leaf. Lay a piece of paper over a piece of leaf; rub your hand over the paper/leaf layer to ensure the leaf sticks to the paper. Lay the leaf on the project surface. Rub the paper backing; remove the paper. Wipe away loose leaf with a soft brush.

FOUR Seal the project surface with varnish or other sealer the leaf manufacturer recommends.

Credits and Resources

Sensible Chic Episodes and Inspiration Room Designers

To see more rooms designed by the professionals listed below, visit HGTV.com/designers

Lesson One, pages 14–21
Episode 702
Designer Val Fiscalini
Val Fiscalini Design
11 Forest Trail
Petaluma, CA 94952
Phone: 707-762-4300
Fax: 707-762-1931
E-mail: valfiscalinidesigns@yahoo.com

Lesson Two, pages 22–29
Episode 703
Designer Joseph Hittinger
Joseph Hittinger Designs
378 Cambridge Ave., Suite B
Palo Alto, CA 94306
Phone: 650-322-8388
Website: www.josephhittingerdesigns.com

Lesson Three, pages 30–37
Episode 704
Designers Jo Ann Hartley and Jennifer Hershon
Hershon/Hartley Design Group
92 Louise St., Suite D
San Rafael, CA 94960
Phone: 415-459-4004
Fax: 415-485-1097
Website: www.hershonhartley.com

Lesson Four, pages 38–45
Episode 706
Designers Sharon Daroca and Eleanore Berman
Design 2
90 Great Oaks Blvs., Suite 103
San Jose, CA 95119
Phone: 408-284-0100
Fax: 408-282-4280
Website: www.design2interiors.com

Lesson Five, pages 47–53
Episode 705
Designer Annie Bowman
Sunrise Home
831 B St.
San Rafael, CA 94901
Phone: 415-458-1937
Website: www.sunrisehome.com

Lesson Six, pages 54–61
Episode 708
Designer Alison Whittaker
Alison Whittaker Design Inc.
Phone: 408-358-8988
E-mail: ahwdesign@aol.com
Website: alisonwhittakerdesign.com

Lesson Seven, pages 62–69
Episode 712
Designer Penny Chin
Elements in Design
Phone: 650-595-8884 or 888-595-8884
Fax: 650-595-2884
Website: www.elementsindesign.com

Lesson Eight, pages 70–77
Episode 709
Designer Jeanese Rowell
Jeanese Rowell Design, Inc.
308 Bryant St.
Palo Alto, CA 94301
Phone: 877-323-1066
Fax: 650-323-1067
E-mail: jrdesign1@mindspring.com

Lesson Nine, pages 78–85
Episode 711
Designer Jeanese Rowell
See above for contact information.

Lesson Ten, pages 86–93
Episode 713
Designer Linda Applewhite
Linda Applewhite and Associates
828 Mission Ave.
San Rafael, CA 94901
Phone: 415-456-2757
Fax: 415-485-6062
E-mail: lappledes@aol.com
Website: www.lindaapplewhite.com

Sensible Chic Design Coordinator
Jen Jordan
E-mail: jenjen@speakeasy.org

The Ultimate Sensible Shopping Guide

Page 10

Chairs, from left: Classic Contemporary Chair, Triangular Back, 17.74" wide x 32" high, 19" diameter. Hawley & Company, www.hawleycompany.com. Froggy Side Chair FR4990 in Chrome, 21" wide x 31" high, 22" diameter. Dauphin, www.dauphin.com.

Page 133

Light Fixtures, from left: Arts and Crafts Pendant in Weathered Bronze, 16" wide x 18" high x 56" tall. Bellacor, www.bellacor.com. Arts and Crafts Collection, 22" wide x 35" tall, 22" diameter. Progress Lighting, www.progresslighting.com. Clatstop Mission Single Pole Art Glass Dome, 22" wide x 22" tall, 31" diameter. Rejuvenation, www.rejuvenation.com.

Pages 134–135

Sofas, from left: Horizon. Rowe, www.rowe.com. Luc Sofa. Mitchell Gold, www.mitchellgold.com. Mansfield Sofa in #219-303. Thayer Coggin, www.thayercoggin.com. *Cross-Section Sofa photo courtesy of Rowe.*

Pages 136–137

Dressers, from left: Hand-painted chest. Jane Keltner, www.janekeltner.com. Hand-decorated Bombe Chest, Swedish Home Collection. Ethan Allen, www.ethanallen.com. *Ethan Allen Chest photo courtesy of Ethan Allen.*

Pages 138–139

Rugs, from left: #3350, Regal-Keshan, 5'x8'. Capel, www.capelrugs.com. Caswell Collection, Design 5687, Navy Sarouk, 5'x8'. Lowe's, www.lowes.com. #9250, Martha's Vineyard, 5'x8'. Capel, www.capelrugs.com.

Pages 140–141

Quilts, from left: Ocean View Napping Quilt, 48" x 72". FunQuilts, www.funquilts.com. Four Corners Quilt. Garnet Hill, www.garnethill.com. Ocean View Napping Quilt *photo courtesy of FunQuilts. Bedding, from left:* Lyric Flat Sheet in Ivory, 500 thread count. Peacock Alley,

Style by the Aisle: Great Chain Stores

Look to these mass merchandisers for budget-savvy furnishings and accessories.

Bed Bath & Beyond
800-462-3966
www.bedbathandbeyond.com

Bombay Company
800-829-7789
www.bombaycompany.com

Burlington Coat Factory Warehouse Corporation
800-444-2628
www.coat.com

Container Store
888-266-8246
www.containerstore.com

Cost Plus World Market
310-441-5115
www.costplus.com

Home Depot
800-553-3199
www.homedepot.com

IKEA North America
800-434-4532
www.ikea.com

Kmart
1-866-562-7848
www.kmart.com

Lamps Plus
800-782-1967
www.lampsplus.com

Linens 'n Things
866-568-7378
www.linensnthings.com

Lowe's Companies, Inc.
800-445-6937
www.lowes.com

Marshalls
888-627-7425
www.marshallsonline.com

National Furniture Liquidators
415-643-8888

Pier 1 Imports
800-245-4595
www.pier1.com

Ross Stores
800-945-7677
www.rossstores.com

Target Department Store
800-800-8800
www.target.com

Tuesday Morning Inc.
972-387-3562
www.tuesdaymorning.com

Wal-Mart
800-925-6278
www.walmart.com

Z Gallerie
800-358-8288
www.zgallerie.com

www.peacockalley.com. Checkerboard Percale, #7856, 250 thread count. Garnet Hill by Wamsutta, www.garnethill.com. Blue Dots. Target, www.target.com.

Pages 142–143

Window Treatments, from left: The Madison Drape in Silk Taffeta, Celadon, 84". Silk Trading, www.silktrading.com. THAI silk drapes, #1320.0028, Lichen Green, 84" long. Restoration Hardware, www.restorationhardware.com.

Pages 144–145

Lamps, from left: Nelson Lamp, 30" tall. Jonathan Adler, www.jonathanadler.com. Cream Linen Drum Shade, #544, and Ribbed Ceramic Base, #242, 16" tall. Target, www.target.com. Classic Urn in Chocolate Brown, 1URN-TLCH, and Medium Bell Shade in Golden Beige, 3SQBL-95MD. Jamie Young Lamps, www.jamieyounglamps.com. Faux Suede Shade, #762, and Brown Metal Urn, #254, 19" tall. Target, www.target.com.

Page 146

Photo Frames from left: Target, www.target.com. *middle and right:* Josephs, Des Moines, IA, www.josephsjewelers.com.

Page 147

Glassware, from left: Zoom. Kosta Boda, www.kostaboda.com. Kiwi Crackle Vase, #9604C-13. Blenko, www.blenkoglass.com.

Page 148

Print: Oak Tree, Sunrise by Ansel Adams, 41"x41". Bare Walls, www.barewalls.com. *Frames, from left:* Bare Walls, www.barewalls.com. Custom Frame. Heartland Gallery West, West Des Moines, IA, 515-223-0500.

Page 149

Pottery, from left: Vase, 10" high, matte. The General Store and More, Urbandale, IA, 515-276-7201. Betty Vase, #270, white, 10" high. Garnet Hill, www.garnethill.com. Belly Vase, 10½" tall. Jonathan Adler, www.jonathanadler.com.

Page 151

Pillows: 18" square. JCPenney, www.jcpenney.com.

The Best Merchandise Marts and Manufacturer Showrooms

Check out these exclusive resources for designer-savvy options. Call ahead to find out when these centers are open to the public.

Boston Design Center
One Design Center Place
Boston, MA 02210
617-338-5062

Chicago Merchandise Mart
222 Merchandise Mart Plz
Chicago, IL 60654
312-527-7939

Kitchen, Bath and Building Design Center
300 D St. S.W.
Washington, DC 20024
202-646-6118

New York Design Center
200 Lexington Ave.
New York, NY 10016
212-679-9500

Pacific Design Center
8687 Melrose Ave.
West Hollywood, CA 90069
310-657-0800
Note: The public may browse, but you must buy through a designer.

Seattle Design Center
5701 6th Ave. S.
Seattle, WA 98108
800-497-7997
Note: Open to the public for browsing in the afternoon; purchases must be made through a designer.

Showplace and Galleria Design Centers
2 Henry Adams St.
San Francisco, CA 94103
415-864-1500
Note: Public-opening policies vary by showroom.

Internet Resources

This is a sampling of the furniture and home decorating resources you can find online. For links to even more catalogs and websites, log on to www.shopathome.com or www.catalogues.com

www.allposters.com
As the name indicates, this site sells inexpensive wall decor. Pieces are available unframed, framed, or mounted—a much less expensive choice than framing under glass.

www.artfulstyle.com
Original paintings, photographs, and fine crafts, including a large selection of objects under $250.

www.ashford.com
Name-brand accessories in traditional styles at up to 50 percent off retail every day.

www.ballarddesigns.com
Furniture and accent pieces with Southern style and a feminine flair. Frequent sales make much of this merchandise affordable for buyers on a budget.

www.brandsmall.com
The basic pieces available at this site will help create the core of a room, but you'll probably want to add more distinctive pieces from other sources to make your room stand out.

www.chiasso.com
Furniture and accessories with a sleek, chic European look. Prices vary, but you'll find something on sale at any time.

www.thecompanystore.com
They started out as a great source for down comforters; now, this "company" sells a wide range of bedding and home accent pieces, and the company reduces prices frequently.

www.domestications.com
Bedsheets, rugs, and accent pieces on this site vary widely in quality (read the fine print for information on fibers and construction), but you can get some super deals.

www.dowahdiddy.com
Do Wah Diddy sells fabulous finds from the '50s and icons of American kitsch at very reasonable prices.

www.eziba.com
Artisans from around the world are represented on this comprehensive website. Whatever your style, you can find an offbeat accessory here.

www.greatwindows.com
From blinds to swags, this site offers window treatments custom-made to your window's measurements. A great option if your windows are not standard sizes.

www.homedecorators.com
A huge selection of wool rugs with plenty of lamps and accent furnishings as well.

www.magellantraders.com
Accents from around the world. Some are pricey, but there are plenty of bargains too.

www.millihome.com
This textile site offers a passage to India—Indian fabrics made into pillows, throws, and table linens—all at very reasonable prices.

www.novica.com
In association with the National Geographic Society, this website offers reasonably priced accessories from around the globe.

www.overstock.com
When manufacturers make more of an item than they can sell through traditional channels, they have to unload it somewhere. That "somewhere" is here—and you can find quality merchandise for more than 50 percent off suggested retail.

www.pearlriver.com
Be sure to visit Pearl River's crowded-with-great-buys store next time you're in New York City's Chinatown. In the meantime, shop for woven wicker floor mats, paper-shaded lamps, and Asian ceramics on the company's website.

www.potterybarn.com
With a wider selection of large furniture than the bricks-and-mortar outposts, the Pottery Barn catalog and website, and the spin-offs Pottery Barn Kids and PB Teen, offer basic furniture and versatile accent pieces.

www.wallkandy.com
Exotic photographs of locales from Venice to Vietnam, sold framed or not, are a great, inexpensive way to add foreign intrigue to your decor.

www.westelm.com
Simple lines and standout colors distinguish this line of furniture and accessories.

Project Resources

Pages 154–155
Paint: Biscuit 6112 (base coat), Tatami Tan 6115 (faux leather). Sherwin Williams, www.sherwinwilliams.com.

Pages 158–159
Top and Bottom Row Ribbon: 1¹⁄₂" sage (#5812680), ⁷⁄₈" charcoal (#5807169), ³⁄₈" gray/blue (#5811369). Center Row Ribbon: 1 ¹⁄₂" charcoal (#5807334), ⁷⁄₈" gray/blue (#5811799), ³⁄₈" sage (#581247). Offray, www.offray.com.

Pages 160–161
Faux Suede: Animal Print #5017, Black #5813, Woodhue #319. Field's Fabric, www.fieldsfabrics.com.

Pages 166–167
Toy Chest: Stack A Shelf Storage Chest. Stack A Shelf, www.stackashelf.com. Tissue Paper: Paper Reflections Jungle Tissue Combo. DMD Industries, dmdind.com.

Pages 170–171
Roller Shade: June Tailor, www.junetailor.com.

Pages 176–177
Paint: Delta Ceramcoat Acrylic Paint in Grape, Royal Fuchsia, Opaque Yellow, Ultra Blue, and Pumpkin. Delta, www.deltacrafts.com. Spray Paint: Krylon Metallics in Bright Silver. Krylon, www.krylon.com.

Pages 178–179
Rug: Seaside Rug in Natural. Home Decorators Collection, www.homedecorators.com.

Pages 182–183
Aluminum Sheets: ArtEmboss Aluminum Light. ArtEmboss, www.artemboss.com.

Index

to some, inspiration comes naturally.
for the rest of us, may we suggest a good book?

HGTV
HOME & GARDEN TELEVISION

BEFORE & AFTER DECORATING

SMART IDEAS TO TRANSFORM EVERY ROOM OF YOUR HOME

HGTV
HOME & GARDEN TELEVISION

DESIGN ON A **DIME**

ACHIEVE HIGH STYLE ON A $1,000 BUDGET

When you're done with *Sensible Chic*, try these other great books from HGTV. In both books, you'll find simple and affordable design ideas, not to mention plenty of inspiration from HGTV's expert designers. *Design on a Dime* highlights 21 smart designs, each with only a $1000 budget, while *HGTV's Before & After Decorating* gives you 32 amazing room makeovers with a minimal investment of time and money.

YOU SHOULD SEE WHAT'S ON **HG**TV !